# WHEN
# A PARENT
# IMPOSES LIMITS

*Discipline, Authority, and Freedom in Today's Family*

*Beth Michel*

# ABBEY PRESS
St. Meinrad, Indiana 47577

COVER: Freelance Photographers Guild/Lettau

Library of Congress Catalogue Card Number
81-68517
ISBN: 0-87029-178-5

# CONTENTS

# Preface

When we were expecting our first baby, I asked my mother when I should begin disciplining our child. "The day he or she is born," my mother answered. I really didn't know what she meant until we had several children, but by that time I better understood the purpose of discipline in anyone's life, and so better understood how the setting of limits could be introduced into an infant's life from day one.

Now, from the perspective of over twenty-three years of child rearing, and from additional experience with other people's children as a Girl Scout and Blue Bird leader, Junior Great Books leader, and teacher at the elementary, secondary, and college levels, I am convinced that discipline, if it is to be meaningful, cannot be begun too early, must be constant, and should pursue three goals.

First, discipline should help children to develop internal controls, to become self-disciplined individuals. Second, discipline should produce individuals who can balance their own wants and needs against those of others, either in the family or in other groups. Finally, discipline should help children adapt to the requirements of social institutions in the larger world.

Discipline, or the imposing of limits on the behavior of ourselves or others, is essential to the living of a fully human life. Discipline, properly rooted in authority and effectively administered, enhances the freedom of the individual. I have found that there are three major problems for parents in the disciplining of their children.

The first problem arises when parents discipline children only as an exercise of parental authority. A second problem develops when parental discipline is administered in a manner that is ineffective or inconsistent. And when permissiveness is the prevailing attitude of parents in dealing with their children, a third major problem is encountered.

This book will discuss the three purposes of discipline, look at the major problems that can develop, and end with a discussion of how to set limits while still encouraging personal growth.

As I write this, I am reminded of a conversation with a friend, the mother of five very active children. We were talking on the telephone against a background of noise and confusion from her end of the line. From time to time, she would cover the mouthpiece, shout something, and then turn back to me. After one particularly loud exchange, she said to me, "Can you believe it? I told Tim three minutes ago that if he hit his sister again, I'd break both his legs. And do you know, he just hit her?" "Surely," I said, "you don't think he thought you meant it?" There was a silent pause. "I guess he didn't," she said. We both laughed.

Discipline is no laughing matter, but neither is it bone breaking in nature. Rather, discipline is the tempering of the child's curiosity with the parent's wisdom, the offsetting of the child's ignorance with the parent's factual appraisal of reality, and the pacing of the child's creative responses to the world with the parent's desire for a child's healthy growth.

CHAPTER ONE

# Encouraging Self-Discipline in Children

The three-year-old son of a friend of mine approached the bridge table where we were sitting, paused a moment to listen to the chatter, and then announced: "I want a little piece of quiet!" Most parents would agree that "a little piece of quiet" is most desirable—and needed. How to achieve this is often a problem, a problem many parents attempt to solve through a coercive form of discipline. How many children are marched off to their rooms so that parents may have "a piece of quiet"? How many games stopped, activities interrupted for that elusive "piece of quiet"? I believe discipline that is designed to produce optimum living conditions primarily for the parents will not at the same time produce optimum growth conditions for the child.

If, when setting limits for our children's behavior, we think first of making our own lives easier or more pleasant, we will develop a different system of discipline than if we think first of what kind of adults we want our children to become. The mother who forbids her toddler to explore those fascinating pots and pans is choosing an orderly kitchen and less work for herself, over a learning experience for her child. A father who can't tolerate any kind of music he himself does not enjoy, and won't have it played in the house, is choosing his taste over the natural desire of his children to be part of the fads and fashions that are so important to their adolescent peer group.

The parent's action in each of these instances produces a negative effect on the child. Toddlers who are allowed to explore, to satisfy their curiosity about shapes and sizes and colors and sounds and textures in safe, if disorderly ways develop a positive attitude toward learning. Toddlers who are forbidden to explore, who are most approved when they are least active, see learning as a risky experience—touch that and get slapped! Teenagers who are not allowed to follow even the innocuous fads of their peer group are prevented from developing the ability to eventually make their own decisions.

While that "piece of quiet" may be longed for, it should not be the goal of discipline. Rather, the goal should be the ultimate self-discipline of the child. When that goal is reached, the home environment will support many "pieces of quiet," emotional quiet as well as physical quiet.

The first step in establishing a system of discipline which will aid the child in developing his or her own internal controls is to look upon discipline as a positive force rather than a negative one. Discipline is to enable, not forbid; discipline is to free, not limit; discipline should be positive, not negative. When parents *and* children realize this, the battle is half won.

Positive discipline goes beyond saying "No." It is easy to say "No." It is often extremely difficult to make that easy "No" stick. "No" is a word that draws a line between two people and dares one of them to

9

step across it. How many times has a simple "No, you can't do that" escalated into an all-afternoon confrontation between a parent and a defiant child? Having issued an ultimatum, one is stuck with defending it. The amount of energy used to defend a "No" often simply isn't worth the reward of obedience that may finally be achieved.

How does one turn a "No" into a positive force? By augmenting the "Nos" with "But you cans." Add "Here's why" to that, and children will become cooperative and willing to respond.

"Here's why" means we explain to children the reason behind our rules and regulations. And the "Here's why" begins when discipline does — in infancy. True, infants cannot understand the meaning of words they hear. They do however understand the feelings communicated. When a parent talks to a baby mentioning that the bottle is still too hot or the corner of the table sharp, when parents explain the limits they set, their reasonable, explaining tone of voice will begin to develop in the baby a positive acceptance of their concern for his or her well-being.

When children realize that the rules and regulations in our homes are for their protection and enrichment, not their limitation, they will be much more motivated to follow them. Discipline that is protective is discipline that sets forth reasonable rules to protect the child from physical harm — don't ride your tricycle in the street, don't get in a car with a stranger; from mental harm — set aside a time for homework each day, study before a test; and from emotional harm — don't rush into intimacy with someone you don't know, don't lie, don't cheat. The reason behind rules, in a system of discipline geared toward producing an internally controlled individual, is the protection of the child. Limits are set to enable the child to grow and develop, not to deny or take the joy from living.

An infant arrives as a totally selfish being. Its strongest felt needs are physical—to be fed, to be warm, to be dry, to be held. And, as every parent knows, an infant will work strenuously to have those needs met. Discipline begins as we gently teach the infant that its needs will be consistently met. In my experience with five babies, early complete attentiveness to their needs assured them that they were cared for, and they became much more relaxed in their demands. Because they were not allowed to go hungry and did not have to scream and scream for food, within a few weeks they no longer cried when it was time to be fed. They woke up, made those soft "I'm awake" sounds, and looked around in peaceful expectation. Of course, my part of the bargain was to consistently be ready to feed them. I considered that an easy bargain to keep, and I had my "piece of quiet" instead of the nerve-wracking yells of a starving and anxious baby.

The parent who creates a crib or playpen environment for the infant in which learning is stimulated by providing the infant with objects to look at, touch, and explore is building the foundation for discipline. As the child grows and is able to crawl, to stand, to walk, and is therefore able to reach and grab for items, the parent introduces the idea of ownership. "This is for me," the mother says, taking the glass vase from the baby, "and this is yours," handing the baby the rubber ball. Personal property is more than a cornerstone of law: it is a cornerstone of discipline. When toddlers begin to understand "mine" and "yours," and respect that distinction, it is easier to teach them to leave other people's property alone.

Toddlers are old enough to begin to understand the reasons for the setting of limits. Two year olds love to pull out pots and pans, but every mother knows that no two year old will have the attention span to put away more than three or four pots. So when three or four pots are pulled out, shut the cabinet doors and say firmly, "Now play with those. You can have more when you are finished with these and put them up." If the child demands all the pots, the parent's task is clear. "You may play with all the pots, only not at the same time. If you want another pot, choose one of these to put back before you take another one out."

Confining a child's activities within the limits of his or her capacity makes good sense. However, it is essential in raising children with the ability to discipline themselves to expand these limits whenever possible. It is one thing to realistically encourage our children to stretch themselves to meet challenges. It is quite another to carelessly allow them to become involved in situations which we know, after a little thought, are beyond them.

A confident son may assure his father that he can feed the neighbors' three dogs while they are on vacation. But if the father knows that his son's physical strength, memory, and enthusiasm are limited, and that he himself will be feeding those three dogs in a matter of days, he will help the child face the reality of the situation and deal with it. "Have you thought how you're going to manage that big sack of food?" "How will you keep the dogs from getting out?" "How will you feed them when you are at baseball practice?" "Are you willing to do this everyday for two weeks?" Self-disciplined people know as much about the kinds of things they should stay out of as they do about the kinds of things they do well.

Two important areas in setting limits for pre-school children are eating and going to bed. The child who eats at regular times, who is given balanced, nutritious meals, is laying the foundation for a lifetime of good health. The child who goes to bed at approximately the same time every night, whose body is allowed to develop an inner rhythm of rest and activity, will be less nervous, more alert, and in a better mood, than the child whose bedtime is open for bargaining.

There is a definite pattern to learning, a definite order. The best time for learning to take place is when the child is ready to learn. A noted child psychologist has written that the "best time to learn" may occur only fifteen or twenty minutes a day, but that if a caring adult can capitalize on those minutes, optimum learning will be possible.

When the baby is ready to learn to feed him-or herself, that is the time to let go of the spoon. I have never understood why children get yelled at for spilling milk or dropping plates while adults who do the same thing are excused. Toddlers spill and drop things because they are uncoordinated, they have short attention spans, and they don't see, at first, the relationship between their hand opening and that puddle of milk on the floor. If a parent reacts strongly to the toddler's spilled milk and food or to the broken plates, the toddler has just been handed a weapon. He or she learns that this all-powerful parent can be controlled just by dropping a glass or a plate. No child should ever be handed that sort of weapon.

When the inevitable spills occur, the cleanup should not be accompanied by anger—"What a bad baby!"—or self-pity—"Look what you did. Now poor mama has to clean it up. Aren't you ashamed?" It is essential that the child suffer the consequences

13

of his or her behavior, and not the adult. When this happens, the behavior will stop. If the parent becomes angry or unhappy because of the child's behavior, who then is suffering the consequences?

The toddler who is beginning to drop food as a game needs to have the plate and spoon removed—firmly! "It's too bad you don't feel like eating now," the parent might say. "Here's a piece of cheese," or wienie—or whatever. "Eat that so you won't be hungry." And then take the child out of the high chair, take off the bib—mealtime is over. And it stays over until the next regular meal. If the parent relents and serves "lunch" at three in the afternoon because the toddler chose to throw the first lunch on the floor, the child will not learn self-discipline. Over and over, psychologists and learning theorists have emphasized the importance of the first three years of life. There are certain learning experiences that the child must have in this span. If these are missed, the child will be lacking in self-discipline.

The guiding principle for early discipline is expressed in these three words: "Leave emotion out!" This is extremely difficult. Yet, if parents can manage, most of the time, to deal with the anger, the rage, the dislike they so naturally feel when encountering a stubborn, time-and-energy-consuming child, without expressing it to the child, the results will be good for the child and for the parent.

This is not to say that children should never be exposed to parental anger and frustration. Even parents who put superhuman effort into leaving emotion out of their discipline will slip enough times for the child to learn that anger is a normal feeling, and that we all express it.

Much of the antisocial behavior of teenagers, including drugs, alcohol, crime, and pregnancy, can be traced to faulty discipline in which the parents made emotion-laden responses to early-childhood behavior such as: "Now look what you've done to Mommy," "You'll make Daddy cry if you do that," "If you love me you won't do that." A child must take personal responsibility for the consequences of behavior. If the child learns that his or her behavior controls how the parent feels about his or her own life, then when the rebellions of adolescence begin—and they will begin, no matter how loving and stable the home—the anger against parents, which is part of this rebellion, may result in a desire to hurt the parent. The teenager may think that the parent is the one harmed when the teenager is arrested for having drugs, gets pregnant, or engages in antisocial behavior. That is the harm done to the child when parental discipline is based on emotion rather than reason.

Discipline that is rooted in reason, the setting of limits with explanations, allows the *child* to suffer—or enjoy—the consequences of his or her own choices and behavior. And this is how positive growth in self-discipline happens.

I have said to my children many, many times: "I want you to know that if you ever choose to experiment with drugs, or get pregnant, or take careless chances in the car, you, not I, will be the one who suffers. You will be in the delivery room, having a baby—I will be in the waiting room. I may very well be crying, but I will have friends to support me, and I will walk out and go home. You will have to decide what to do about the baby, and you will have to live with that choice. If you land in jail, I will come see you. Again, I will be in pain, but I will be free. I can go home, go to work, do whatever free people choose. You will have a record; there will be certain

15

careers and life choices that you will never have open to you. If you drive recklessly, or ride with people who do, and are maimed, scarred, or killed, I will certainly weep. I will never really get over it. But you will have the useless arm or leg, the scarred face — or death." These words seem terribly harsh and unloving. I believe that they are the most loving words I can say to my children, because I say them to impress on them, as powerfully as I can, that the person who suffers most from a choice or is most rewarded by it is the one who makes and carries it out.

It may seem tempting to make choices for our children — don't we know a great deal more about life than they do? And, in some instances, we certainly do have to make the choices. But ordinarily, we should work toward helping the child to make and carry out choices, choices that are life-giving for him or her, choices whose positive consequences the child will experience.

Let me share an example that demonstrates that the person carrying out the choice, not the person who makes it, suffers the consequences or enjoys the rewards.

The instance deals with a young man who, when he finished high school, wanted to study music. His father, an extremely rigid and authoritarian person, said that he would not pay for his son's education if he majored in music. It was not a question of money, the father was highly successful in making money. The boy began college enrolled in predentistry. And then the long years of carrying out his father's choices for him rather than learning to make his own culminated in rebellion when the son realized that his father was choosing something for him that would affect the rest of his life. The son got into drugs, exhibited severe personality disturbances, and ended up in an intensive therapy program. His parents were divorced during all of this — the father's authoritarian approach did not stop with the children. When the son came out of treatment, he was able to start over. He is now majoring in music, keeping himself and his life in order — and benefiting or suffering from his own choices.

A parent cannot decide upon a life for the child to live. From infancy the parents' task is to guide the child in taking responsibility for his or her own choices. That is what discipline is all about.

CHAPTER TWO
# Setting Limits in the Family

Almost everyone has seen the Boys Town poster that depicts two boys, one carrying the other on his shoulders. The caption reads: "He ain't heavy, Father—he's my brother." As parents, how we all long for that kind of love to exist between our children! And how often we feel that just the opposite exists.

Sibling rivalry will always exist in families, no matter how hard we try to be "fair" in dealing with our children. A friend of mine, who is married to a psychiatrist, had her two children eleven months apart. They thought this spacing would reduce the first child's negative feelings when the baby arrived. As it happened, both children are boys. My friend and her husband have always tried to be "fair" with their two boys. Yet she told me recently that her two sons, now both in college, came to her and complained about that very thing. "Why are you always so fair?" one said. "Yeah," said the other, "why can't you show a little favoritism?"

It is the desire to be first that sparks sibling rivalry. And that desire rarely dies. It may diminish, but it cannot—because of the very nature of human beings—completely die. Almost all family arguments: "It's mine!" "It is not!" or "You let him do it. It's not fair!" are rooted in this desire to be first, to be special. Often, antisocial or antifamily behavior is the child's way of getting attention — to be, for however short a time, first in the parent's eye, even if that eye is red with rage. It has been unhappily noted, that time and time again abused children, even badly abused children, will choose to go back to the abusive parent rather than stay with a kind but nonparent person. *Any* attention from a parent seems to be better than no attention.

A discipline system based upon respect for others: for the property of others, for the time of others, for the effort of others, and for the results of those efforts, will produce a family atmosphere in which quarreling, fighting, and hostility among children is reduced to a tolerable level.

In Chapter One, we discussed how to initiate toddlers into such a system of discipline. This is done by setting limits in a nonemotional manner and then explaining these limits and offering alternatives. As the toddler grows, and particularly when there are other children in the household, the process of relating to other people, of becoming socialized, begins. The setting of limits on an individual's behavior is an essential part of this learning process.

*Positive socialization — the ability to get on well with others while not denying one's own individuality — begins with the recognition of property rights, our own and those of others.* Almost the first "social right" the child challenges is the right to property. "What's mine is mine and what's yours is mine, also" is the undisciplined attitude of a young child!

As toddlers, children need to begin to develop the idea of "mine" and "yours." A rule in family living should be that no one borrows, uses, or in any way disturbs property belonging to another family member. I know of families in which children lock their room doors when they leave the house because they don't trust their brothers and sisters not to invade them and carry off whatever strikes their fancy. We have had instances of one daughter borrowing an item of clothing or jewelry from another without the owner's permission. In those instances, we have backed the owner. I've been appealed to by a daughter wanting to borrow an absent owner's sweater or blouse, or whatever, to give my permission. My answer is that I cannot give permission when I do not own the item in question.

We have rules governing the lending of such things as clothes and jewelry outside of the family circle. I feel that parents should not have to work to provide a special dress or a nice wardrobe for their child, only to have someone else wear it, and perhaps ruin it. This may seem selfish. But if children are allowed to lend the items their parents have provided, they do not develop a proper sense of ownership and the responsibilities that go with ownership. Our daughters have been told that they may lend to their friends the clothes or items that they pay for, but not the ones that we pay for. In this way, they are choosing to lend something which they not only "own" in that it was purchased for them, but that they "own" in that they paid for it. This has led to a more discriminating approval of borrowers.

This attitude of respect for the property of others, and respect for one's own, can be instilled by example first and discussion later. If a child leaves a toy in the yard and it is likely to be ruined by the weather, do not leave it outside to teach the child a lesson. Rather bring it in and return it to the child: "Here is your new doll; it was left outside. I know this doll is important to you and I want you to have it, so I brought it in." This deals with your respect for your child's property. Now explain to the child the consequences of his or her carelessness if property is not respected in the future: "If it rains on your doll it could ruin it. I know you love your doll and don't want this to happen. I am concerned because you're having difficulty remembering to bring in your toys, and yet we agreed that you would take care of your things. What do you think would help you be less careless?"

Such an approach is nonjudgmental. The child is not told that he or she is careless, ungrateful, lazy, or driving the parent crazy. The child is not made to feel unlovable or rejected, as can happen when the person rather than the behavior is dealt with. Second, this approach is firm. It leaves no room for bargaining on the original agreement, which was that the child would take care of his or her possessions, but it does allow for the sharing of ideas. The parent says that what he or she has tried hasn't worked— what ideas does the child have? This implies that the parent and the child are sharing the problem, as, in reality, they are.

Naturally, some of the ideas the child has as to how the situation can be improved will be absurd, maddening, perhaps even insulting. It is important to not judge the ideas, but to simply encourage the expression of as many as possible, and then evaluate how well they meet the problem. The important thing is that the child learn to respect property.

It is a difficult task on the one hand to give our children a certain quantity of "things," and on the other to teach them the relative unimportance of these things in their lives. What needs to be understood, I think, is that it is not ownership of property or enjoyment of property that is destructive of spiritual values. What is destructive is when a person identifies his or her life or being with what he or she owns or possesses. When we draw our sense of self-worth from material things, then spiritual emptiness begins. It is possible for children to grow up owning and enjoying a fair amount of material goods and at the same time have solid Christian values. But if our children are to survive spiritually, they must be able to resist the terrible materialism of our time; they must know that "I am what I think, believe, and do" not "I am what I own."

In our family, what we have done as parents is tell our children, and, I hope, show our children, that we truly believe a person's worth lies in how they live, not where they live. Our daughters know that no matter how much money is available, there are and always will be certain limits on how much will be spent on "things." They know that we believe that the most important gifts we can give them are: first of all, faith in God; second, the strength of character to live that faith; and third, values that make that faith real. These gifts are theirs for all eternity.

This is not to say that our children neither own nor enjoy property. They certainly do. But I see no signs of destructive materialism. I can't remember hearing them put down people because of their clothes, or their street address, or because they don't belong to a certain social group. I have heard moans about having nothing to wear, when there are several new outfits hanging in the closet. I have had daughters weep because their hair looks terrible, even though they just blew their allowance on having it done. But as a woman, I know there are times in a woman's life when she could have the showrooms of the top New York designers in her closet, and she would still have nothing to wear. There are times when everyone we meet says our hair is gorgeous, and we still think it looks like the kitchen mop. To counter those times when doubt and insecurity conquer us, there are, happily, those times when we wear a five-year-old dress and know we look great.

Material goods simply do not have the power to make us feel better about ourselves if, at bottom, we live with self-doubt. If it were possible to buy confidence, we would buy it. But when we try to buy confidence under the guise of a certain garment, car, label, makeup, or any other thing that lies outside of ourselves, we are doomed. A healthy respect for property recognizes property as just that—something that lies outside of ourselves.

In teaching children to respect property, we teach by the way we take care of our own property and that of others. Further, we teach children what property can do, and what it cannot do. A car can provide transportation, in varying degrees of luxury, and with varying degrees of efficiency and cost. It cannot do more than that.

Over and above the normal possessions which most children have, there is the problem of property involved with hobbies, interests, and activities. Tremendous strain can be put on the family budget by the ever-changing interests of children. Even if a family could afford a never-ending stream of camera equipment, tropical fish supplies, sporting goods, or records, it is certainly not in the best interest of the child to purchase everything asked for, even in such a good cause as geology or microbiology.

Setting limits on how much of what to buy can put parents in a dilemma. A parent will naturally want to encourage a child's interest in positive activities such as photography or painting. When the alternatives to constructive behavior are as destructive as those available to our children, we often feel pressured into going overboard to support the things we see as "good."

But there can be too much of a good thing. Children need to learn that, while we do want them to develop interests and have hobbies, we also want them to develop a sense of financial responsibility. We want them to know the price, and we want them to know how to choose whether to pay it or not.

If children are guided to assume all responsibility for hobby equipment's use and care (all that they are physically capable of) and as much of the financial responsibility as they can reasonably handle, we are not nearly so liable to end up with closets and attics and basements filled with the goods of abandoned interests. In this way, the child will not only appreciate the efforts the parent initially made in securing the item, but will also gain an appreciation of the personal effort needed to replace it.

The first time a hobby, interest, or activity is proposed that will require a significant expenditure, we need to discuss the question of responsibility with the child. The child needs to understand what duties and maintenance responsibilities he or she will have — and these can range from feeding the new gerbils to keeping the new car washed — and what financial responsibilities there will be. Maybe we will buy the gerbils and the cage, but the child will provide the food. Maybe we will help with the car's down payment and half the monthly payment, but the son or daughter pays the rest, plus gas, oil, maintenance, and insurance. When one daughter got a tropical fish aquarium at age eight after eighteen months of wanting one, we bought the tank, filter, and pump, as well as a set number of fish. She bought the food and replacement fish. I did the initial cleaning of the tank, but she had to help me until she learned and then it was her task.

It is always wise to go into hobbies gradually. If we agree to buy a camera and a developing tank and a lot of other darkroom equipment for a novice photographer, we are almost asking to be stuck with used goods that have almost no resale value. Most hobbies, interests, and activities can be begun with limited expenditure — even musical instruments can normally be rented for the first six months.

*A second task to accomplish in learning how to get along well with others is to learn to respect time, your own and that of others.* How does respecting time fit into a system of discipline, of setting limits? Primarily, by encouraging self-control, independence, and consideration of others. A person who possesses these qualities is a disciplined person, in the truest sense of the word.

I know mothers who spend their time trying to meet the demands of their children's involvement in a variety of teams, school activities, jobs, and social clubs. These women may make ten trips a day, may serve dinner staggered over three hours, and may literally have no time for themselves. No matter how healthy all this activity is for the children, it is not at all constructive of their characters for them to learn that their time is more important than their mother's. From being accepting children, they may very well turn into highly demanding adults, who believe that anyone involved with them should automatically give up time to meet their needs and wants.

Having raised five children in a city with inadequate public transportation, I have certainly done my share of driving and catering to erratic work or play schedules. One summer I did indeed make ten trips a day, but that was the last time that I did. It seemed to me that my children would learn far more about the value of time, theirs and mine, if they had to choose among activities, and then be responsible for their own time when they were not so involved. As they got older, and it became more difficult to regularly have family dinner together, I opted against running a cafeteria with continuous service. We settled on a nightly dinner hour that best fit our schedules. Then, if someone was unable to be home for the meal, that plate was filled and kept warm. There might have been as many as four plates being kept warm, but at least I could clear away the rest of the dinner and get out of the kitchen at an hour that protected my leisure time.

Of course one reason many parents are so willing to give up some of their time to take their children to lessons and team practices is that they do not then have to face the ever-recurring question: "What can I do?" I believe another gift we should give our children is the gift of being able to handle leisure time. They will never learn to do this if they don't have any!

Learning to respect time includes accepting responsibility for keeping the curfew a family sets.

Our youngest daughter was having a great deal of trouble in coming in on time. Finally, we asked her to help find a solution. When many ideas had been discussed and rejected, two solutions were left. One was that all house doors would be locked and bolted, so that she would have to get one of us up to let her in. The other was that the front door would be locked but not bolted, so that she could use her house key to get in. She was then to come to our room and tell us she was home.

She preferred not to be let in "like a baby" and chose to come tell us she was home. The fact that she hasn't had any difficulty in living up to the terms of her curfew says to me that her tardiness was, indeed, nothing more than carelessness about time, and not a deliberate breaking of a family rule.

I think this is important. Too many parents start a war when there is no enemy in sight. It is destructive to the trust that should exist between parent and child to automatically assume that every negative act of the child is deliberate. If the child is being deliberately negative, then help of some kind is definitely needed. An occasional deliberate breaking of a family rule isn't a sign of something serious, but certainly a pattern of deliberate negative behavior is. In such a case, punishment by the parent will do little good. It is necessary to uncover the root of the negative behavior.

When a family rule is violated, as it was in the case of our daughter and the curfew, the parents should discuss with the child possible solutions to the problem.

Once a solution has been agreed upon, it is probably wise to give it a trial period to see if both parent and child can live with it. Few things convince a child more that family rules are really made for his or her own welfare than learning that parents are flexible. Note that flexible does not mean weak, inconsistent, or easily persuaded. It simply means that the parents are open to new situations and new conditions, that the parents realize that the rule about no dates on school nights might very well be suspended if the biggest rock star of this century is appearing one night only, and that night happens to be during the school week. Inflexible rules don't consider people, their needs or their wants. And I don't think we can convince others that we love them, truly love them, if we do not consider what they need, and what they want. At the same time, children must learn to respect the needs and wants of parents.

For a long time, until our youngest child was eight years old, the hours between one and three on summer afternoons were "rest time." Even when no one was taking a nap, the children were expected to be in their rooms, reading, writing letters, whatever. But that whatever had to be quiet! Told by my children that they didn't need rest time, I replied that I did. The children came to respect my need. Those two hours were my "piece of quiet" that restored me for the rest of the afternoon.

Learning to handle time is especially important as children enter the higher grades. There are many opportunities for after-school activities that present scheduling problems. How can the child be in two clubs and on one team and still have time for homework? How can the child have a paper route and still sing in the choir?

In helping the child answer these questions, it is necessary to teach the child how to set priorities. When we know what is most important, or most necessary, it is usually easier to know how much time we can devote to each activity.

Unfortunately, parents and children often do not agree on which activities are more important! The child will give football the nod over homework every time; same with cheerleading practice. It is the parents' duty to guide the children when their own immaturity makes them shortsighted.

So long as a child is in school, going to school and preparing for going to school is that child's "work." Just as the parents have their work to earn money to support the family, to make and maintain the home, the children have their work. Just as an employed parent has a boss, a superior, or his or her own standards to satisfy, the child has teachers. And just as the future security and stability of the family depends on how conscientiously the parents do their work, the future security and stability of the child's life depends upon the child doing his or her work — the work of getting an education.

Our children have all been told this from the earliest years. They have understood that their education is our responsibility to provide but their responsibility to acquire. They have to meet the standards of their school, not we. They have to take the consequences of homework not done, tests failed.

The value of this approach is that it helps the child set, very early, the top priority in his or her life — getting an education. Consistently reinforcing and encouraging that priority will not reduce the child's reluctance to put schoolwork ahead of play, but it will make the decision less of an emotional battle.

I have taught at the elementary, high school, and college levels, and there is no question in my mind that those students, who truly believe that an education is one of the most valuable assets they will ever have, learn, regardless of the teacher or the learning situation. Parents can find in their children's report cards evidence of the effect motivation has on learning — the highest grades are almost always earned in the subject in which the child is most interested. If the child is convinced that all subjects are important, that everything studied will ultimately contribute to his or her life as an educated person, then grades should improve in all subjects.

Opportunities to help the child prioritize his or her time come when the child begins formal education. Other tasks the child has—feeding a pet, emptying wastebaskets, folding laundry—will have to be worked in around the demands of education. The kindergartner meeting a bus or car pool may have to get up fifteen minutes earlier to make sure the cat gets fed or the dog gets walked.

I think it is essential that the child learn about priorities as soon as demands of unequal importance exist. Further, the child should learn to take responsibility for meeting those priorities. We learned fairly early that chore charts, made out on poster board and hung in the kitchen, were a great help in accomplishing this. The children always had input into the making of these charts. We took into consideration which afternoons they had club meetings, music lessons, or other activities, before deciding which day they would perform which chore or chores. They always opted to have one day when they did more in order to have at least one free day. Part of the agreement was that if a child could not, for some reason, carry out a chore on a chosen day, that child had the obligation to swap with someone else or pay another to do it. I found that the children were better than me at enforcing whose turn it was. If most of them were being reliable, they came down pretty hard on one who wasn't.

I think it is vital that when chores are assigned, children do have input as to when they will do them. In order for children to learn to be in charge of their own lives, they need to be able to test their judgment at every safe opportunity as they are growing up. Many times, a daughter, from my perspective, would leave folding the clothes until very late in the evening. According to her point of view, she was waiting until she could combine watching a favorite TV show with folding the clothes. When I realized that it was the sight of those unfolded clothes piled in the kitchen that bothered me, we solved the problem. Any clothes that weren't folded by dinnertime were simply taken to the folder's bedroom, to be folded at the time she chose.

We did not leave up to the children's choice, however, the standard of performance expected. Each family has its own ideas about what constitutes a properly cleaned kitchen or a properly folded load of laundry. It is important that our children learn what our standards are and live up to them. The old maxim that taking the easy way out makes more work in the long run is usually truer for sloppily performed household chores than for almost any other activity.

In learning to respect time it is important to not only be able to assign time to activities in order of importance, but to allow enough time for each activity. It is in this second area that children need a great deal of guidance. Very few people are able to go through a day, allotting exactly the correct amount of time to each thing they have to do. It is possible to learn to assign time and to conserve time, so that order is imposed on even the most hectic schedule. Basically, this comes from experience as we learn just how much time a given task takes. This is learned through trial and error. Perhaps we first set aside an hour to mow the lawn. We know now it takes two hours and twenty minutes. By sharing the fruits of our experience with our children we can help them learn to allocate their time, but experience remains a most valuable teacher.

When we teach our children to respect time, their own and that of others, we are giving them a tool that will discipline their lives, and, through that discipline, set them free. People who know how to control time are never slaves to the clock!

*A third step of positive socialization is for the child to learn to respect the efforts of others.* I know of no way to more thoroughly ruin a child than to let him or her grow up with no respect for the work that other people do. Children who do not respect the work of others when they are young will have very little respect for their own work later, with disastrous economic and social results.

How many of us know parents who wait on their children hand and foot, making the beds of hulking teenagers, cleaning the kitchen after snacks, rescuing clothes from the bottom of the closet, reminding of books to be returned to the library? This has negative effects on both parent and child. The parent becomes the lowest form of help, the unappreciated self-sacrificing martyr. The child becomes an ungrateful tyrant. Not only do such children not learn anything about taking care of themselves, they conclude that parents exist only to work for the child. They have no respect for what the parent does for them, for they have come to view it as their right. Such a view makes them ungrateful and self-centered, hardly qualities that enhance their ability to get along with others.

Many parents do their children the disservice of treating them this way because the alternative of getting their children to do the chores themselves seems so difficult. But children can be taught and motivated to do their chores. There is a system which does work, is unemotional, does put the child in charge of his or her life, and does help the child accept the consequences of his or her own choices. I call this the "with privilege goes responsibility" system. It is certainly nothing new — and it has worked within our family.

Until age five, none of our children had any routine chores. At age five, however, they entered the world of work. Their first chore was to make up their own beds. That, plus keeping toys picked up, putting clothes in the laundry, and *one* general family chore, such as setting the table, was considered a sufficient introduction to work. I would always pick a "special" time, perhaps a tea party for the two of us, to discuss these new responsibilities with the five year old. I would point out first that being five meant more than just going to kindergarten, it meant being old enough for a few new privileges. These privileges always included staying up half an hour later. I then dealt with whatever special wishes that particular child had. One child was given the privilege of having a pet, another the privilege of taking music lessons. What is a privilege to one child isn't necessarily a privilege to another.

When the child understood that being older meant more privileges, I would explain that, in our family, with privilege went responsibility. Being five years old meant staying up a half hour later, but it also meant making your own bed. My daughter was now expected to make her bed every morning. I would still change the sheets, but ordinary bed making was up to her. (At first, it was difficult to resist remaking those lumpy beds, but I soon decided that when a daughter was tired of sleeping on wrinkled sheets, she would learn to pull them smooth.) I also discussed the other tasks the child would do. The five year old was usually delighted to be included on the "big girls" chore chart, at whatever cost.

When I was sure we both understood what new privilege and also what new responsibilities the child had as a result of being five years old, I would explain that if the child decided she did not want the

33

responsibilities of being five, and demonstrated this decision by routinely not performing her tasks, I would then assume that she did not want the privileges, either. It was perfectly all right with me if she preferred to be four, to have her bed made up for her, her clothes hung up, and to be taken off the chore chart. But, as a four year old, she certainly could not expect the privileges of being five.

This system may sound like a power game or a trap. It is not. The most balanced adults are those who thoroughly understand and accept the consequences of their own choices. If we choose to act immaturely, we will have certain consequences to face — and these are rarely pleasant. It is immature to choose to behave in a manner appropriate to an age younger than we really are, whether our real age is five, twenty-five, forty, or fifty. It is a mark of maturity to act your age, in terms of wisdom, judgment, and reliability.

Of course the child will forget to do chores, or will test the system. If only carelessness is involved, if the child has really bought the idea that privileges come with accepting responsibility, a few reminders should be sufficient. If, on the other hand, the child is testing the parent's dedication to the system, the child should be told that since he or she has chosen not to accept the responsibility of being five, he or she is not to be surprised that the privileges that go with the responsibility are now being removed. The child is free, at any time, to choose to be five again. Until that time, his or her life will revert to the responsibility level and privilege level of a four year old.

Whatever the age of the child, the principle applies: Responsibility and privilege go together.

In helping our children learn to respect the efforts of others, we teach them by getting them involved in the effort of maintaining their own lives. By attaching certain privileges to certain responsibilities, we teach them to respect work and those who work.

*The final component in a positive discipline system that helps a child learn how to socialize with others is learning to respect the results of the efforts of others.* These results include everything from the items purchased with the income earned by the employed members of the family to the food prepared for the family by whomever does the cooking.

As in so many areas of discipline, example is the best teacher. As soon as young children are aware of the world around them, and begin to interact with that world, they also begin to pick up the attitudes and behavior patterns of those in their immediate environment. Children who grow up in homes where the cook is complimented on the meals, where those who care for the house and yard are thanked for the order and beauty created, where those who provide income are thanked for the clothes, toys, movie tickets, and school fees, grow up into appreciative adults.

Children are taught to respect the results of others' efforts when children are taught to care for the things made for them or purchased for them by someone else. Children have little idea of the value of money—how long or how hard a parent had to work to earn the sum that purchased the new jacket, the new bike. There is a fine line between laying guilt on children for being such an expense and giving them a realistic idea of the share of the family income that is, indeed, spent on them. It can happen that love and money become confused in the child's mind: the child equates parental love with parental generosity.

When that occurs — and in our family it did occur — it is necessary to deal with the underlying problem. There is no one way to help a child accept the fact that parental love should not be measured by how much money the parents are willing to spend to gratify the child. Nor is there any one way to help a child see that when a parent mentions money already committed to the child as one reason for not immediately committing more, the parent is not trying to make the child feel guilty. When the child remains confused, professional help should be sought. In no instance should parents allow this sort of confusion to continue.

One effective method of helping children learn to respect the results of others' efforts, a respect which evolves into respect for the results of their own efforts, is to give them some valid reasons for taking care of property. What parent has not been angry and frustrated at seeing almost new, still good toys, clothes, or athletic equipment ruined through carelessness or total indifference? And what parent has not faced the dilemma of wanting not to replace a certain item to "teach the child a lesson" but having to replace it if the item is some essential thing? I know there are parents who would, for example, no longer allow their child to play on a team because a uniform shirt was lost or a baseball glove stolen. I really think absolute financial impossibility of replacement is the only reason this should happen. The difficulty of fitting the punishment to the crime is one of the reasons I'm not strong on punishment.

Somehow or other, we hit on the idea of really leveling with our children as to why they should take care of their property. There really are only two reasons for taking care of things — one is economic and the other is sentimental. We should take care of property because it will cost us something to replace it, or we should take care of property because we have an emotional attachment to it.

I learned, through trial and error — the children's trial and my error! — that reminding our children constantly of the hundred different reasons that came to my mind as to why they should be more careful with things wasn't one bit effective. What finally was effective was to state the true reason: "We have a certain amount of money to spend on recreation in our family," I would say. "Your play things, such as the new wading pool, are bought with some of that money. If you are careless, and punch holes in the pool, we will buy another one, because we want you to play in the water. But the new pool will come out of the money that is set aside for your recreation, and so you won't be able to do some other things. For instance, if we have to buy a new pool, in doing so we will spend the money that otherwise could have been spent on going to the movies." This same reasoning applies to clothes, athletic equipment, or other such personal items.

It is no good to yell at a son that he is going to have to go without a Windbreaker when winter is coming. We know very well we will not let him go without one. If we use as punishment the phrase, "I will not buy another," aren't we saying to our children that we weren't very discriminating buyers in the first place? Either the child needed or wanted the item, and we agreed that he or she needed or should have it, or else a foolish purchase was made. If the child did need or want the item and we originally agreed with that need or want, and if we can financially replace the item, what sense does it make not to replace it? What does make sense, it seems to me, is to help the child see that the more money that is spent on replacing or repairing destroyed property, the less is available to spend on future wants or needs.

When an optional purchase is suggested by the child, it is the time to point out, not as an "I told you so" but as a sobering fact of life, that the money that could have been spent on this adorable new blouse was spent, unfortunately, to replace the sweater left at the basketball game and never recovered. When the optional purchase is very close to a child's heart, is very much desired, I see nothing wrong in working with the child to help him or her buy the item. Not with a "loan," or with a "gift," but with opportunities to earn the money through honest work. Far greater than the material goods we give our children is the realization that we are not doomed to commit the same mistakes over and over, that one error does not put heaven beyond our reach, that through our own efforts, we can do better, be better, and live better.

* * *

If a child is to live a satisfying life and develop into a well-rounded, mature adult, he or she needs from an early age to learn how to get along well with others. By setting limits and positively disciplining their child, parents are fostering this learning. In dealing with self and others, if a child respects property, time, efforts, and the results of effort, he or she will have a solid foundation for positive social relationships.

CHAPTER THREE
# Becoming Socially Acceptable

A friend of mind attended a women's convention in Chicago. Letitia Baldrige, who re-edited Amy Vanderbilt's classic book on etiquette, spoke at one of the luncheons. She told the assembled women that she is kept very profitably busy teaching new high-level employees of large New York firms the intricacies of etiquette. Men and women with degrees from M.I.T., Harvard, and equally impressive universities have the technical knowledge for their positions, but not the social knowledge so vital for work with firms who consider knowing which fork to use almost as necessary as knowing how to read a financial statement. Teaching children good manners, so that they will be socially acceptable, is an essential part of the discipline required for children to adapt to larger social institutions.

Good manners require that we control our primitive and natural instincts, that we put the feelings of others on at least as important a level as our own, and that we make ourselves attend to the courtesies that still, in this informal age, separate those who know how to live graciously from those who do not.

When parents teach children to have good manners, the quality of life in their homes improves dramatically, and the children get a great deal more from their school experience, from field trips, from attending the theater, from travel, from dining out, from visiting and being visited. Far from being an imposition on their freedom, good manners are a gift our children will use all their lives.

If we fail to teach our children good manners, we will probably receive many complaints about our children's behavior outside the home; we certainly penalize our children as they seek a place in the wider world; and we will have to spend a lot of time with rude people. If we fail to impose limits on behavior in the home and allow rudeness and bad manners, we should know that our children are likely to be seen as rude, disruptive, noncooperative, or hostile by teachers, theater ushers, waiters, librarians, flight attendants, salespeople, and others with whom our children must deal. Further, well-mannered children are welcome guests in the homes of their friends, and are better hosts when friends visit them.

There are, it seems to me, two categories of manners. First, there are the manners that equip children to deal with people of all ages in all sorts of relationships and in all kinds of situations. These manners have a certain flexibility. Depending upon the personality of the child, their use will vary creatively, but the essence of the courtesies observed remains the same. It is good manners for a child to respect older people. A child is taught this principle, but then shows his or her respect differently depending on whether the older person is a grandparent, neighbor, or school official. The second category of manners equips children to deal with certain formal situations in life that do have established routines which are recognized almost universally.

**The first category of manners** is concerned with such details of everyday living as eating with people; answering the door or the telephone; conversing with guests of other members of the family; introducing friends to relatives or to other friends; participating in public or private entertainments; traveling by private or public transport; going to school; making use of libraries, museums, art galleries, planetariums, zoos, concert halls, and the like; and being a good guest and a good host.

"All that!" the dismayed parent wonders. Yes, all that. My favorite line from that marvelous musical, *My Fair Lady,* is Professor Higgins's answer to Eliza's charge that he is rude. "I am not rude," he declares. "I treat everyone exactly the same!" That line contains a kernel of truth that makes the "all that" of manners far less complicated than a first look would lead us to believe.

When our children learn to treat everyone the same, in terms of interpersonal courtesies, we do not have to give extensive lessons or admonitions before each new visit or each new experience. The child's own awareness of what is courteous and what is not, of what sort of behavior respects the rights of others while at the same time protecting his or her own rights, will allow the child to make decisions about manners that will leave everyone feeling well treated. There are even courteous ways to vehemently disagree with someone; courteous ways to terminate employment, a friendship, an engagement.

I want to make it clear that in talking about good manners, I am not talking about behavior which is too often designated "manners." Such behavior looks artificial, practiced, "prissy," superior.

41

It serves as a mask, so that the real person never emerges. True manners are never a mask. They may help us to conceal personal feelings best left unexpressed at that moment, they may help us maintain our dignity through difficult encounters, but they are never false, never artificial, never put on with our best dress because we are going to a party. Certainly, manners are used in degrees—table manners at the family dinner table should be good; table manners at an elegant restaurant or more formal meal should be excellent—but there shouldn't be a dramatic change.

I remember well how I was taught good manners in my family. I can remember that when I was about three and my older sister was about six, my mother invited us to tea at least one afternoon a week. She would extend the invitation in the morning, asking us if we could have tea with her that afternoon at three o'clock. We learned to give her a definite answer, one which made it clear that we knew what we had been invited to, and at what time we were expected. That afternoon, we would wash our hands and faces, brush our hair, see that our shoes were shined and our dresses clean, and go outside, walk up the sidewalk, knock at the door, and be greeted by our hostess. She would have tiny sandwiches prepared and small cakes or cookies, all arranged on some of her loveliest plates, and the tea would be steeping in a pretty pot. There would be cloth napkins, careful handling of cups and spoons and saucers, small talk, and a proper leave taking with thanks to the hostess.

My first experiences at these tea parties consisted largely of learning to manage all that paraphernalia! But as time went on and I became at ease, the pure enjoyment of sharing tea and talk took over, and I made a step forward in learning why parties are fun. I began staging these tea parties early with my own daughters, and having tea together has remained a favorite activity. How many happy hours we have spent drinking tea and talking! This spring, one of my girls suggested having a tea for young mothers and their small children. I wish you could have seen those teeny people, from age three to age seven, really enjoying a tea. Our children are far more appreciative of gracious living than we may think. While I have no sons, my house has been filled with the sons of my friends, and, as the girls got older, with the boys that gravitated to them. I have seen enough well-mannered boys who were also terrors on the football field to know that boys can take pleasure in being well mannered.

Teaching manners at home consists primarily, I think, of two things. First, an atmosphere must be created in which mannerly behavior is the only appropriate behavior. Second, parental example must be consistent.

Let's talk about creating an atmosphere that seems to require mannerly behavior. The unfortunate tendency for the family meal to become a movable feast has done much to work against this type of atmosphere. If family members drift in and out of the kitchen according to the TV schedule, if meals are eaten standing up at the telephone or sitting in front of the television set, or in a bedroom listening to the stereo, there is no possibility for learning manners or anything else.

Even the most chaotic family schedule should allow for at least one night a week when everyone can be present. Young families should be able to have many more family meals together. I know that some parents, in an effort to have better conversation between themselves, feed the children first and have an "adult" meal on their own. The feedback I have gotten from my children when they visited homes where this was the rule convinced me that children, even very young children, know when they are being excluded, and don't like it. Naturally, there are times when parents should be able to have an adult meal, but if family is important, if well-behaved children are important, then the family dinner is essential. I know of families in which the father's work schedule goes well into the evening. These men regularly come home for the family meal and then go back to the hospital, the office, the store, or whatever. If the distance between work and home doesn't allow that, a parent's late hours still don't have to preclude a shared meal. Even if it is necessary for children to eat early, they can at least come back to the table and have dessert with their parents.

Why do I stress this so much? Because when children eat with adults regularly, when attention is paid to them, both in the conversation and in the way the meal is prepared and served, they are motivated to want to be included in more of these pleasant occasions. And when they are told that a desired pleasant occasion does have a few behavior rules that go with it, they are much more willing to live with the limits so as to enjoy the experience. This pleasant occasion becomes an opportunity to teach not only table manners but also conversational courtesies and courtesies that have to do with punctuality and consideration of others' feelings — all important in becoming socially acceptable.

The time to teach proper eating methods — don't chew with your mouth open or talk with your mouth full, don't hold food in one hand and a fork or knife in the other, don't leave your spoon in your coffee cup or tea glass — is when the child is very young. Correcting children about manners while they are eating isn't pleasant for anyone, and yet, if we don't correct the act when it occurs, how will they learn? At each stage of learning to eat and to handle various utensils, the child should be told the proper way. It helps to repeatedly explain that the most important reason to eat in a mannerly way is so as not to offend one's fellow diners. I remember one friend of mine who in desperation propped a mirror in front of her recalcitrant son at every meal. His manners improved greatly!

Of course, families differ in the degree of table manners they require. But it is well to remember that no one can be too well mannered, and that poor manners are not only socially, but economically detrimental. The parents' goal should be to help children become self-disciplined, well-adjusted adults who can function well in most of life's situations. To effectively impart this message, parents themselves need to be consciously aware of their own manners and seek to improve them.

Manners are habits. Everyone has some bad habits. I think that as children grow older and have mastered basic good table manners but still have some bad habits, all we can do is give reminders after the meal, away from the table, and let it go at that. Mothers have discovered to their amazement that a sixteen-year-old girl achieves more in bringing out the Sir Galahad in their sons than all their years of nagging, and the same mothers have nearly fainted when someone calls to say what beautiful manners a sloppy daughter has.

Other aspects of appropriate table behavior are conversational courtesies, punctuality, and consideration of others. Any parent knows that, after a child has achieved a certain competence in language, his or her idea of conversation may be to recount an entire episode of a television show, the whole plot of a movie, or a greatly detailed account of an argument with a friend. And so, along with setting limits on what sort of behavior is appropriate when eating, we also need to set limits on what is conversation and what isn't.

Most people would agree that conversation is an exchange of ideas, thoughts, feelings, anecdotes — that it is not a monologue, an attack, a diatribe, or an ego trip. While some people may hold that any topic is appropriate to any circumstance, I firmly believe that, while all topics should be able to be discussed in family life, there are some topics better discussed away from the family dinner table. Families normally have their own list of acceptable dinner table topics: what is considered highly interesting to a family living on a ranch might be considered unpleasant to a family living in a city.

In our home we use a signal when a discussion is getting too personal, or when a topic doesn't seem appropriate to some family member. "Not of general interest" is a phrase someone picked up somewhere. It wasn't long before instead of saying, "That's not of general interest," someone would just say, "No G." And if enough others agreed, that topic was tabled.

Our family dinner table is the scene of lively conversation, ranging over many subjects. We have tried not to let it become an arena for sibling fights, for parental lectures, or for causing younger members to feel educationally and conversationally inadequate. My husband and I tried to make sure that each of five eager little girls had a turn to share her day, and as they all went to the same school and were all very close in age, the facial expressions of sisters waiting their turn to give their version of some exciting event were hilarious to behold! As they got older, and began to discuss issues and ideas, the heat as well as light shed upon the subjects could produce a great deal of warmth. But I must say we were never bored, and, as they began to bring friends home for dinner, we got reactions that still make me laugh. One young man, born and reared an only child in New York City, came for a Sunday night dinner at which all five sisters were present, ranging then in age from twelve to twenty. He was very quiet during the meal. Later the daughter who had brought him said he asked her, "Is it always like this?" But he did come back.

A very firm rule in our house is that when family dinner is announced, the TV and stereo go off, the telephone is hung up, and everyone comes to the table on time. It doesn't take a great deal of effort to check the TV schedule before mealtime to see if some really special program conflicts with the normal dinner hour. If it does, a compromise can be made. But we have never believed that any sit-com was as important to our children's growth as having dinner with the family. Now that several of our girls are at college, I am more and more grateful for the hours we spent creating our own dialogue instead of listening to someone else's.

Chapter Two discussed in great detail teaching children to respect the property, the time, the effort and the results of that effort, of both themselves and others. This respect, once taught and accepted into the child's character, makes learning courteous behavior much simpler, for courtesy, it seems to me, is nothing more nor less than an outward sign of our respect for ourselves and others.

Children with that kind of respect will not destroy public or private property when they go to school, libraries, museums, movie theaters, or anywhere else. Children with that kind of respect will be social beings who take care of the books, furnishings, and play equipment at school, who understand that the teacher's time and effort does require their respect if not their approval, and who respect the right of their classmates to study if they wish, to be able to hear the teacher if they wish, without disruptive behavior from another student. How truly sad it is for a young child to earn an undeserved reputation for being "bad" in school, when he or she is only ignorant of courteous social behavior.

When our children have mastered courteous methods of dining with others and conversing with others, and when these skills are added to a healthy respect for property, time, effort, and the results of efforts, we will have, I feel, children who can and will profit from every educational, cultural, athletic, social, or travel experience they have, and, at the same time, bring a great deal of pleasure to others.

**The second category of manners** deals with certain formal life situations in which there are established routines, routines which, when observed, do create a positive image about the child's upbringing and manners. This would include such things as writing letters and thank-you notes, issuing and responding to invitations, being a guest and being a host, recognizing important events in the lives of friends and relatives, wearing proper attire for certain occasions, and, in general, doing all of those things which seem onerous to do until we have to suffer the consequences of either not knowing to do them, or knowing, but failing to do them anyway.

Most children are initiated into "social" life when they are invited to a playmate's birthday party.

And, unfortunately, this initiation sometimes convinces the child to be antisocial the rest of his or her life. When very young children "entertain," it is obviously up to the parent to set the standard of courtesy. Courtesy requires that no guest be made to feel badly because his or her gift isn't as "good" as someone else's, or is a duplicate, or isn't liked. The birthday child must have the good manners to thank each guest, not to compare gifts, and not to choose only one special friend with whom to share a new toy. I have found that if all the gifts, once opened, are picked up and put away, with a game or food being introduced immediately, a lot of tears are avoided.

Courtesy also requires that no guest be made to feel rejected because he or she can't run as fast as another guest or pin the tail on the donkey as well. I had birthday parties for each of my five children every year that they wanted one, which meant up to about sixth grade. We never had games in which there was one-on-one competition, one winner or a definite loser. We had a lot of team games, including elaborate treasure hunts and creative dramatics, and both teams always won a prize.

I can almost promise that if you will locate two highly creative and enthusiastic teenagers to run the party, you will be amazed at the results. It may cost you lunch for two at one of those fancy hamburger places, but it will be worth it.

What parent has not dreaded a teenager's request for a party, knowing that alcohol or drug use, heavy petting, or worse might well result, or that "crashers" could cause havoc? We found that having older teenagers on hand at our children's parties helped avoid many discipline problems.

We recruited older boys who had some status with the younger set. I have never yet seen a four-teen-year-old smart aleck who would keep on disrupting a party after an eighteen-year-old football player went over and told him to stop. As the age of the guests rose, our recruited chaperones got older — and those college boys brought home by older daughters were very valuable in spotting suspicious behavior and bringing it to a halt. All I had to do was stay in the kitchen and keep the food going, enjoying the reports these young men brought of what they had just told some rotten kid.

We accepted the fact that when teenagers drove to the parties, they were likely to have beer or liquor in the car. As they came in the front door, my husband or I would say to them, "There's a tub of ice next to the tub of soft drinks. If you want to put your beer in that, it'll taste better. There's nothing much worse than hot beer." This statement was greeted with a variety of reactions. But I assure you, once that beer was safely in the house, it rarely got touched! The kids were so busy eating, talking, listening to music, fiddling with the chess sets, puzzles, and games, that just happened to be lying about, that we usually inherited several six-packs after each party. And that in-and-out-to-the-cars business simply didn't happen. With five girls, and I don't know how many after-play, after-game, after-concert, or just plain parties, I can only remember one guest who had too much to drink, and he was twenty-two.

Another limit we set, once the girls reached the slumber party age, and later, the teen party age, is this: If you are old enough to have this kind of party, you are old enough to prepare for it and to clean up afterwards. If this means you recruit your friends to help, fine, but I will not sweep up popcorn and chewing gum wrappers after a slumber party, nor pick up paper cups and napkins after a dance. I will help cook, I will serve the food and drinks, I will stay up to the bitter end, but I won't do the cleaning.

The only sad note we have had in years of having houses full of kids is the number who come to us and say, "Gee, my mom would never let me do this." Maybe there are kids who destroy houses, but we haven't had them. Another reason for rearing self-disciplined children is that as teenagers, they're less likely to make friends with the ones whose behavior is outside of the limits our children have come to comfortably accept.

Another formal rule of social living is the practice of writing thank-you notes for gifts. The only way to train children to write thank-you notes is to do it with them in the beginning. Even very young children can dictate a note to a grandparent, a godparent, or a friend. Some of the most wonderful thank-you notes I have received are from a godson, who very early began composing his own. He would never let his mother, a dear friend of mine, see them, and she was constantly amazed at the sincerity and originality of what he wrote.

Our third daughter is named for an aunt of mine; she and this lady have a deep relationship despite the almost seventy years that separate them. My aunt told me that one of her most cherished possessions is the note that accompanied the pillbox her namesake at age five sent her for Christmas. "Dear Aunt Marjorie," the note said. "I got you this little box because you are an old lady and I think maybe old ladies get faint and need a pill and I wanted you to have a pretty box to put yours in. Love, Marjorie."

The practice of writing notes and letters is one that has been, to a great extent, lost in our society. But those who take the time to write can bring so much joy, so much love, so much warmth, into the lives of others, that it is a practice well worth helping our children develop.

There are also formal rules about important events in the lives of friends and relatives, events surrounding births, weddings, serious illnesses, and deaths. Each region of the country has standards for what is proper and what is not; ethnic groups have their own rituals that celebrate or bring solace. Our children should be familiar with what is done in the area in which they live, as well as what is appropriate in the wider world. How many misunderstandings, hurt feelings, and broken friendships would be prevented if only more people had an understanding of the basic courtesies required for weddings and funerals. Libraries and bookstores have many excellent etiquette books. A family would do well to get such a book for the children to read and study, and adapt what it says to their lives.

While I do not believe in exposing very young children to the reality of death and the funeral and burial, I do believe that part of our job as parents is to help them understand, as well as they can, what has happened and what they can do for the bereaved.

In our own grief, we sometimes forget how sensitive children are. When my father died of cancer, I was talking with my four year old, who was devoted to him. "It's better for Pops," I said. "He would never have gotten well, and he is with God." "That's fine about Pops," she said, "but what about Mama?" (My mother.) That, of course, is the very heart of the matter about the courtesies offered to the bereaved. When we teach our children to have the discipline to think, not of their own aversion to death, or funerals, or grief, but of the pain of those who have lost someone, we will have done them a great service. And we teach that kind of behavior best by exhibiting it ourselves.

A final word on setting limits that will help our children adapt to social institutions deals with proper attire for certain occasions. It is almost laughable in these days of creative dressing for any parent to think he or she can exert much influence on what children wear. And, if we wait to exert that influence until the children are teenagers, we probably will be engaged in one long battle after the other.

Here again, instruction in what is proper attire for certain occasions begins at an early age, as early as two or three. Instead of taking our young daughters shopping with me, I would select a number of dresses or pants or whatever that I considered appropriate for kindergarten or church or birthday parties, and that we could also afford. I would take them home, tell the child involved that she could choose two or one or three, or whatever number I could buy. In this way, I controlled appropriateness, and she still learned to make a decision.

As the girls grew older, there were those frustrating shopping trips that send mothers to convents begging to be taken in, and, because our garment makers seem determined to make our daughters look like women of doubtful morals, there were some battles to fight. I don't know how I hit on this procedure, but it unfailingly worked. When a daughter brought home an outfit that was too tight, cut too low, or otherwise unacceptable, I would first look at it and question just as I did with every garment: "How well is it made." "Will these seams hold up?" "What about that color, will it fade?" "How much is it?" "I wonder if you could find something better made and maybe with better lines." And so on. By

53

getting the daughter to deal with the garment, which she very well knew I would oppose, on a realistic level of "Is it a good buy?" the emotion was taken out and she sometimes decided on her own to take the thing back. If all else failed, their father took over. He would explain, very carefully and directly, why he didn't want a daughter of his wearing a garment like that. He talked more about love and concern and respect for her than he did about what terrible taste she had. When these persuasive techniques were added to what had been a lifelong educational process in what makes a garment worth having, we somehow surmounted most of the trauma of dressing girls.

I recommend that every girl learn to sew. When she knows what good construction, good cut, good line, and good material are, she will be a better consumer.

Some friends with sons tell me that dressing boys is the most futile occupation any mother ever engaged in, that only a large washing machine and a large dryer will save you, and that the only way to know they have at least one decent suit for state occasions is to hog-tie them and make them buy it. Other mothers of sons bemoan the fact that they're as fashion conscious as girls. All of these mothers agree that, once a boy notices girls, he wears whatever his current girl likes.

Our children should know, however, that while clothes do not make the man or woman, neatness, cleanliness, even hems, pressed shirts, do count. And once again, the lessons learned about respecting the property, the time, the effort, and the results of that effort of ourselves and others goes a long way in helping our children discipline themselves in purchasing and caring for clothes.

54

These first three chapters have dealt with a wide range of topics, all intended to help children take responsibility for their own lives and to learn how to properly conduct themselves in interaction with others. The purpose of setting limits on children is to help them form internal controls, to help them balance their wants and needs against those of others, both in the family and outside of it, and to help them adapt to the requirements of social institutions in the larger world. Through the exercise of their authority, parents impose these limits on their children. An understanding of parental authority is necessary for a proper understanding of discipline.

CHAPTER FOUR
# Discipline
# and
# Parental Authority

What parent has not shouted "Because I said so!" when a directive is challenged by a rebellious child. As universal as this statement is, I will risk stating that the true effectiveness of discipline in a family is inversely proportionate to the frequency with which that edict is given. The more frequent the edict, the less effective the discipline.

I listened one evening as a man described his childhood, one in which the ultimate expression of parental authority, physical abuse, was used. "The day I was big enough to hit back was the day they stopped hitting me," he said. Fortunately, he had dealt with the effect of these early traumatic experiences on his life, and had learned to avoid repeating the same patterns within his own family. Even though not resorting to physical abuse, many parents exercise their parental authority solely for the sake of authority. They have a great need to let their children know who is in charge.

"But we do have authority over our children," parents say — and rightly. We are legally responsible for their behavior so long as they are minors. We are legally bound to support them, and we are morally bound to rear them. These requirements assign, and also define, authority. However, we sometimes forget that our authority as parents comes to us from God, that it is in obedience to his will that we perform our parental duties, and that we have no authority to perform those duties in ways that will frustrate the ultimate spiritual growth of our children.

I am firmly convinced that children who obey parents "Because I said so" will not develop their own internal controls, will not experience the kind of spiritual growth necessary to live a moral life, and will be easy prey to other "authority" figures we as parents may not approve of. Cults are formed because people are willing and accustomed to give control of their lives to someone else. No cult leader can order his or her followers to commit violent and inhuman acts, and be obeyed, if those followers have been disciplined to make and be responsible for their own decisions. When a child complains that another person "made me do it," we can be alerted to the confusion that may be developing in the child's mind when he or she is required to do something because father or mother says so, but not when someone else says so. Children accustomed to doing as an authority figure commands often leave home and find other authority figures who run their lives for them.

It is possible for parents to elicit obedience to family and societal limits without constantly resorting to the authority of "Because I said so." Why then do some parents rely on their own authority alone, and what can be the results of such reliance?

A very general statement, but one which is supported by most psychiatrists, psychologists, and other observers of human nature, is that people who insist on being the authority figure in any given situation are usually people who feel insecure and inadequate within themselves. Note that I said—"in *any* given situation." While it is totally appropriate for a surgeon to give commands in the operating room, his or her authority does not and should not transfer when participating as just another person in a group. But, we all know people who can never forget that they are the boss!

When the underlying inadequacy or insecurity that compels such claims to authority is neurotic in origin, the individual, obviously, will have to have some sort of counseling to deal with his or her problem. But many parents feel inadequate, not because they're neurotic, but because they have never been parents before; nothing in their lives has really prepared them for this awesome role. As the years go by, and the little people with little problems become big people with big problems, parents are truly scared —and rightly so! This sense of inadequacy can be prevented by parenting education, and it is encouraging that so many organizations are beginning to offer parenting programs in which parents can receive support and training before family life begins to suffer.

It is so easy, when a trusting three year old looks up at you, to say, "Because I said so." It is so easy to establish a pattern of "do what I say and you get a reward (my approval or a treat), don't do what I say and you get punished (loss of my approval or deprivation of a privilege)."

When children become teenagers, parents may wish that the simple command "Because I said so" would produce the desired results. "Don't go to an R-rated movie." "Don't experiment with drugs, alcohol, or sex." "Don't drive recklessly." "Don't shoplift." —"Because I said not to!" But it won't work. Children will heed such admonitions only if they have developed internal controls through a system of discipline that has taught them to make choices responsibly.

Some parents rely on parental authority as the "enforcer" because this technique makes them feel more adequate. Others use it because it seems easier. Still others rely on parental authority because they themselves were reared in extremely rigid and authoritarian homes, have never broken out of that pattern of behavior, and so continue it with their own children. Very rigid authoritarians are sometimes projecting their anger that they cannot control the circumstances of their own lives. They compensate for this feeling by attempting to completely control the lives of their families. Almost any upheaval in an adult's life that causes the loss of a sense of control can lead to the attempt to overcontrol one's children.

But we make things more difficult when we rely solely on our own authority. Using this method in order to get children to respond positively to the limits we set can destroy true relating between parent and child.

The first effect of this approach is on the parent. Once we decide that we have the authority to *tell* our children what to do, we begin a process that will eventually undermine our legitimate parental authority. Note that I used the verb "tell." Telling someone to do something is quite different from leading them to do it, guiding them to do it, stating that they will do it, or discussing whether they will or will not do it. Issuing demands leaves no room for flexibility, and discipline must be flexible to be effective. We *tell* our toddler to pick up the toys. When he or she does so, we are pleased—not only with the

59

toddler, who has picked up toys we would otherwise have had to pick up, but with ourselves because we have been recognized as powerful. There is nothing more insidiously destructive than love of power. Gradually, our pleasure in the child's obedience can become not only pleasure that the child is learning to be a civilized and moral person, but pleasure that we have power over someone else. For many parents, the only power they think they have is over their children.

What authority do parents actually have? The authority attached to the parental function, period. And the parental function, according to biblical injunction, is to bring the child up in the ways of God, and to teach him or her to "Render unto God what is God's and to Caesar what is Caesar's." A parent would do well to make it clear to the child that the parent has a duty, imposed by God, to teach, to guide, to lead, to help, and that the parent has the authority to see to it that those teachings, that guidance, that leadership, and that help receive a positive response. But parents cannot force a positive response; we cannot order it. We can only call it forth.

Although love of power is destructive, far more destructive to parents who rely on authority to enforce obedience is the feeling that we are responsible for the lives of our adult children. If we choose, in those formative years, to mold children who do what we tell them only because we tell them to, if we decide to take the responsibility for their behavior, then are we not responsible for the adult child who chooses a course we cannot endorse?

A friend of mine asked me how I could possibly "allow" a nineteen-year-old daughter to spend the summer in Los Angeles studying jazz guitar and an eighteen-year-old daughter to leave for a year of study in France. Wouldn't I worry myself sick? "I want a peaceful old age," I said. "When I'm trying to rock quietly, I don't want middle-aged daughters calling me up telling me they wished I had 'let' them do this or that. They are both over eighteen, their father and I have done all we can do, and now they must be responsible for themselves." I can handle a little authority, so long as I know its limits, but God save me from power over anyone's life!

The effects of an authoritarian discipline system are, of course, just as harmful — if not more so — for the child as for the parent. The child who learns to follow another's lead rather than make his or her own decisions can come to real grief. But an even more devastating consequence is that he or she will lead an unexamined life unless the ability to make one's own choices and decisions has been learned.

The fullest meaning of Christ's great commandment that we love our neighbors as ourselves is that we know ourselves, accept ourselves, and from that self-knowledge and self-acceptance, learn to know and accept others. To know ourselves, we must examine our lives. As our children grow up, they must realize that they have chosen a certain path. And, in examining the reasons for their choice, they will learn something about themselves that they would never have learned had the path been chosen because "we told them so." Perhaps the most freeing moment in the growth of an individual comes when that individual examines him- or herself, sees the faults, the failings, the bad habits — and accepts that he or she is lovable, anyway! In that moment, the individual understands that God does love each of us, warts and all, with a personal love.

Another difficulty with an authority-oriented

discipline system is that the child tends to obey the person rather than live within the limits set by the system. Thus, when the authoritarian parent is away, a baby-sitter, relative, or friend charged with care of the child may find it almost impossible to get the child to go to bed on time, to do homework, or to respond to direction. When the child has accepted the discipline system, however, any care-taking person with the ability to follow the system will maintain the discipline.

I can testify from my own experience that the sitters who cared for our children, whether for an evening, a weekend, or a week, were unanimous in saying that they had had little difficulty in keeping the girls within the limits we had set before we left. This doesn't mean that we are superparents or our children superkids — we are as faulty a collection of seven people as could be found in any family. But our five daughters have been reared in a discipline system that stresses personal responsibility not blind conformity, and offers personal enhancement which leads to full maturity.

Our girls give evidence of having developed internal controls. They are able to make decisions, get to work and class on time, turn in assignments, and choose not to spend time with certain people in certain activities. They live up to the agreements they make with each other and with us, and are fairly responsible about money — both that which they earn and that which we give them. They also have developed a sense of community responsibility and, insofar as their individual maturation levels allow, are willing to take the consequences of their own behavior.

This doesn't mean that all is sweetness and light. It very often is not, but turmoil is part of the natural process of growing up. There are two "crisis periods" when a child's development—mental, emotional, and spiritual—is likely to be particularly uneven. Between twelve and fifteen, they're trying to grow up too fast, and between eighteen and twenty-one, they very often can't seem to decide if they really want to finish "growing up," with all the responsibility that entails. As a friend of mine says about this age group, "They're too old to be so young."

I find that my four older daughters are still torn between wanting the privileges of adulthood—being in charge of their own lives—and the privileges of being children, with mother and father to take up the slack or put back the pieces. Some of our most verbal and angry battles have been over this point, when I insist that they not choose adulthood when it's convenient, and yet fall back into childish reliance on parents when it is not. I am perfectly willing to help anybody any time, when the need is valid and the individual has made a responsible effort. But when I am asked to do something that an adult daughter could have and should have done for herself, when I see that "rescuing" her will only reinforce a habit of relying on me rather than herself, I say, "No," and then comfort myself by telling myself that a mother's job isn't to be popular, it is to rear infants into mature adults.

Where does authority fit in a flexible system of discipline? Earlier in this chapter, I said that "telling" someone to do something is quite different from leading them to do it, guiding them to do it, stating that they will do it, or discussing whether they will or will not do it. When these four quite different communication techniques are used, authority can be invoked, when needed, and it will be effective.

Let's look at these communication techniques.

"Leading" involves personal example. In the chapter which discussed respect for the property, time, effort, and results of effort of both ourselves and others, I commented that one of the principal ways in which we could teach our children to have that kind of respect was to demonstrate, through both word and deed, that we have it ourselves.

In the same way, we can lead our teenagers away from negative influences and toward positive ones by our own example. A friend of mine was horrified one afternoon to hear her four-year-old son using several four-letter words not considered acceptable in society. "Where in _____ did he pick those up?" she said, and was then appalled to realize that when in the company of close friends, she sometimes used language more appropriate to the locker room than to the family home.

When our children see that we live the principles we preach, that we do not support immoral entertainment, that we do not say one thing about the use of drugs and alcohol and do quite another, that we do not vote for men and women who are publicly known to be dishonest—in other words, when they see that we are, to the best of our ability, trying to lead lives that do reflect the value system we have taught them, and, if that kind of leadership is shown throughout a child's life, then even our teenagers will follow. It is very important that our children realize that certain substances, and certain activities, that are appropriate for mature adults are not appropriate for them. The argument, "You and Daddy drink" or "You and Daddy went to that movie," can be countered with the explanation that with maturity comes privilege and that with privilege comes responsibility: To drink only in moderation or to attend "mature" movies or read adult books only after assessing what doing so might do to our own spiritual lives. Our children can understand this, if we are honest enough to express it.

"Guiding" is different from "leading" in that personal example need not be involved at all, except as an explanatory device. Earlier this summer, our youngest daughter found that she had great difficulty in structuring her time to accomplish certain goals she had set. She wanted to paint her bedroom, make new curtains, and refinish her furniture. But somehow, one day after the other slipped leisurely by, and she saw that she had not yet learned to structure available time in order to reach goals.

When she talked to me about it, I listened to her thoughts and feelings of frustration. The plans she was making were going to be as ineffective as having no plan at all, because they involved total commitment to the projects until they were finished, with no time for anything else. Realistically, that would never work. She would become tired, both physically and mentally, long before the work was accomplished. And she would be frustrated, because her attempt to plan the attainment of her goals had not worked.

I talked to her about principles of time and task-management, which begin with breaking large tasks down into smaller tasks which can be completed in a predictable time. I mentioned examples from my own experience: how, when I organize my week, (as I do every Sunday afternoon) I divide what I have to accomplish into segments, determine how long these segments will take, and then work the timed segments into the routine schedule of household and family tasks that I perform every week. I showed her one of my worksheets, with specific tasks assigned to every day of the week. And I pointed out that, even

65

on the most crowded days, I either left blank time for emergencies, or had the tasks prioritized so that, if something more important came up I could drop something less important and not become frantic. (Even with this kind of organization, I have days where everything goes wrong, but at least I can still usually accomplish the top priority task and not end the day feeling completely frustrated.) And I emphasized that every day, every week, should have some "take care of me" time.

This is, I think, guidance. We point out a possible solution, we explain it, and we leave it up to the child how much, if any, of the solution will be adapted and used. Guidance is valuable in situations where there are no moral, legal, or ethical issues involved. After all, if her room wasn't redone, no harm would result. I realize that unfinished projects are the bane of all parents' existence, particularly when the parents have paid for the materials. I think the only way to deal with this situation without starting a year-long war over putting the zipper in that skirt or finishing repairing that motorbike is to firmly and quietly state that, until a parent-supported project is finished, there will be no further financial support for any new project. And then stick to it.

Discussion plays a vital role in maintaining discipline and limits when teenagers are involved. There are so many situations that arise in which potential harm exists, that we very often want to say "No" and just take the anger that inevitably follows. A group trip to the beach, a ski resort, someone's camp, or an out-of-town dance or party calls to parents' minds visions of wild behavior and dangerous conduct, and, unfortunately, most parents of teenagers know enough true stories to make these visions uncomfortably prophetic.

But as our sons and daughters enter adulthood, as they leave the family home, as they get away from watchdog parental control, they will be faced with such situations, over and over again. That's why discussion is so helpful, for in discussing a situation, we can separate what is good from what is bad, or potentially bad, and usually arrive at a decision agreeable to both parents and child.

For instance, the good in a group trip to a beach or to a ski resort is the very real recreational value involved. In almost any social or recreational proposal, there is some good. The harm, of course, can come from the type of arrangements that have been made. The presence or absence of chaperones, and the identity and age of those chaperones, the housing accommodations, the people who make up the group — all of these factors help determine whether the trip or party, is "good" or "bad."

By openly discussing these points, by expressing our honest feelings, and by listening to the feelings our children express about these matters, mutually acceptable decisions can be made. Perhaps we will sanction the trip, having gained assurances that certain conditions will be met. Or seeing the value of our concerns, our son or daughter may choose not to make the trip.

If discussion is open and honest, an agreeable compromise can usually be reached. I remember when one daughter wanted to go to Florida with a group that included the boy she was dating. The first announcement was as casual as these announcements usually are — a group was going to the beach, they would camp out, could she go? But when we actually discussed the trip, I learned that her date's married sister and husband would be along, that all the girls would stay in a camper with the sister, and all the boys would camp in tents on the beach.

I am not so naive as to think that the presence of chaperones, or separate sleeping accommodations, can keep sexually active young people apart. In discussions we have had with our daughters concerning coed trips, we have pointed out that, to many people, the appearance of evil is the same as the evil itself. If they choose to put themselves into situations where there are no planned safeguards, they should not be surprised if people assume that they took full advantage of the situation.

This same daughter was invited to a fraternity dance which was to be held in a hotel in a city over 200 miles away from the university, and her date informed her that she was expected to share a room with him. This, he said, was the custom for most of the fraternities on campus. (Regretably, I learned that to be true.) When she protested such a plan, he said they would occupy separate beds. And he proceeded to tell her how many of her friends and sorority sisters would be there.

She called me and told me about the invitation. We discussed the ridiculousness of his statement about separate beds, and the more we talked, the more obvious it was that she did not want to go, would not go, and didn't care who else did go. She saw that such an invitation was degrading and insulting. She said "No" and heard about it for weeks. Much of what she heard was supportive from both male and female students. She learned something of value. She learned that, through discussion, through thought and evaluation, she could apply her value system to a social situation, could make a decision, and could live with it. Even more she gained in self-respect. Joan Didion ends her essay "On Self-Respect" with these words: "Self-respect is being able to sleep in the bed you made that day." I think all parents of teenagers need to frame this statement, embroider it, decoupage it—do anything to help our children understand what a very true statement this is.

The final communication technique is "stating" that our child will do what we have said that he or she will do. If we have led, guided, and discussed, then on those occasions when we do have to clearly, firmly, and without any possibility of change, say "You will not do that" or "You will do this," the natural authority that accrues to parents who are fair most of the time will enforce that statement. We may be willing to give reasons for our statement, and we may also be willing to express the strength of our feelings. I think it is helpful if we do. But giving reasons and expressing feelings doesn't mean the matter is open for discussion. There are some occasions when no discussion, no compromise, is possible. Because a flat statement of "you will" or "you won't" usually generates hostility and anger in a teenager, I think these statements should be reserved for those times when real moral, legal, and ethical issues are at stake.

Of course, just because we make such a statement doesn't mean it will be obeyed. For that reason, I think it is important that we tell the son or daughter just what consequences he or she can expect if our decision is defied. These consequences may be personal or they may be public. There may be punishment which results as a natural consequence of the act, or there may be punishment imposed by another—the parent, the law, the victim of the act. If a teenager decides to go ahead in the face of all warnings and of all opposition, then the parents have done all that they can in conscience do.

The only thing left is not to feel guilty if the child does run into trouble.

One of the most difficult things for our children to realize is that the self-destructive acts they perform to "get back at us," or in rebellion against authority, ours or someone else's, actually work to destroy them first, and only peripherally others around them. When they grow up with that awareness, they are far more receptive to statements which command. If they can remember ignoring an order to finish the term paper on time and as a result failing the course, if they can remember defying an order not to go out with a certain person and ending up with a warning from a juvenile court judge, they will be more willing to admit that parents do know a little about the world, and that if Mother and Father are not leading, guiding, or discussing, but stating—then perhaps they had better listen. But never "Because I said so!"

CHAPTER FIVE

# Inconsistent
# and Ineffective
# Discipline

A character in a play I wrote — the seventy-six-year-old mother of a forty-five-year-old daughter — says to that daughter, "I had no idea mothering went on forever!" Parents often feel that way about discipline. It is tedious and frightening to realize that every day we must be about the business of making those primitive little creatures living with us into self-controlled human beings without destroying their spirit of curiosity, of fun, of adventure. Because of the constant demands on us as parents, it is easy enough to fall into a system of discipline that is inconsistent or ineffective or both, a system of discipline that will not work.

Inconsistent discipline is common in families. On days when the parent's world is going well, the children can do no wrong, or almost no wrong. On other days, when the parent's world is falling apart, the simplest offense, one that was ignored or smiled at earlier that very week, brings the wrath of the frustrated and angry adult down on the child's confused head.

Discipline may be inconsistent for any number of reasons. Some of these are: the mood of the parent, which child is being disciplined, the situation, and the purpose of the discipline. Let's look at these, at the same time being aware of the inconsistencies in our own efforts to impose limits on our children.

*The emotional state of the parent is frequently a cause of inconsistency.* If there is a parent who hasn't overheard a child saying to a playmate, "I'd better not ask her now, she's in a terrible mood!" that parent is either hard of hearing, never around the children, or a marvel of consistency! Most of us, no matter how well intentioned we may be, have days when any request is just one more burden, and the answer "No" emerges before we have given the request any real thought. While it may not be "fair" to say "yes" one day and "no" the next day to the same request—because one day we feel good and the next day we don't —there are times when the inability of the parent to tolerate one more demand is the most important factor involved in the decision to say "yes" or "no." If the child has been raised to respect the feelings and moods of others, that child will be able to understand and accept occasional emotion-laden, nonthinking parental responses.

If a parent, early in the relationship with a child, lets his or her emotional state control most interaction, if one evening mother calmly sees milk spilled and says nothing, and the next evening she reacts to spilled milk with anger and threats, then a game is being set up. And, since children are extremely skillful game players, a behavior pattern will emerge that will be difficult to break.

There are people whose temperaments are so volatile, or whose lives are so unstable, that inconsistent emotional reactions are regretably to be expected of them. Such a parent should try to talk this over with the child. Even a young child can understand if a hot-tempered parent apologizes, emphasizing that the anger was not at the child, was far too great for the incident involved, and that the parent is well aware of this fault which makes life difficult for those around him or her.

A parent's responses may be inconsistent simply because of the parent's own fears about his or her ability to manage, to carry on. I think children should know this. While it's not necessary or at all desirable for children to know of all the turmoil in a parent's life, it is helpful if the child knows that the reason mother set that really unreasonable curfew was that she herself was going through a difficult time, and was, in that particular moment, venting anger. While explanations of this sort may not prevent the inconsistency, they do make it understandable — and what we can understand, we can at least hope to deal with.

When, for any reason, one parent is inconsistent in discipline because of emotional reasons, the situation should be explained to the child or children involved. While it is more desirable that the parent whose emotions are affecting the child do the explaining, this is not always possible. I would even recommend that a caring relative speak to the child or children, rather than let them live in ignorance as to why their parent or parents were so approving one day and so very disapproving the next.

The real and very destructive harm of inconsistency is that when the child is greeted with alternating approval and disapproval for the very same act and when the child can see no reason for this changing response, the child's security is undermined, his or her world is fragmented, and there is nothing left to cling to. Because the very nature of young children demands parental approval, the child may begin increasingly frantic but futile efforts to make the parent consistent.

These efforts may be conciliatory, with the child developing into an anxious, eager to please person, whose only thought is to get and keep the inconsistent parent in an approving mood. How many children have nursed hypochondriac mothers or placated sulking fathers, in just such hopeless attempts to feel secure, to feel love?

Or the child may take the opposite course and become a little hellion. If I am consistently bad, the child reasons, then perhaps my parents will always respond with punishment. The surety that punishment will follow actually produces less anxiety in the child than never knowing whether his or her behavior will produce a smile or a slap.

A young child is not able to separate his or her behavior from him- or herself: the child is what the child does. The parent needs to help the child make this important distinction. The reason inconsistent discipline is so destructive is that the child really doesn't see that it is the behavior towards which the parent is inconsistent. The child feels that the inconsistency is directed to him- or herself. Parents need to develop the habit of expressing disapproval clearly, in a way that definitely separates the behavior from the child. For example: "I don't like to see toys thrown at people. I like you a lot, I love you, but I still don't like it when you throw toys." We can disapprove totally of the behavior, but still love and accept the child.

*Inconsistency by the parent is sometimes related to which child is being disciplined.* "I would never let Harry drive to an out-of-town game," a woman said to me, "but I let Jim do it any time he asks." Now, if driving to an out-of-town game is a privilege that can be earned by accepting the responsibility of staying within the speed limit, not drinking, and getting home on time, then any child who accepts these limits should be given the privilege. When Harry chooses to accept the responsibility, he should have the privilege. But if there are no clear-cut responsibilities attached to the privilege, then the privilege becomes a gift to be dispensed by the parent at will. When this situation exists, the worst sort of jealousy and ill feeling will develop among siblings.

Favoritism has no place in families. It is rarely true that we love all of our children the same — how could we love very different individuals in precisely the same way? Our treatment of our children, our response to their needs, the way we discipline them, should be based on a system flexible enough to account for individual differences, and yet consistent enough that the children are secure with a sense of equal treatment.

There are times in every family when one child "needs" more than the others. The need may be physical — perhaps illness requiring special care. The need may be emotional — the child may be going through a traumatic time in which, legitimately, he or she requires more parental time and energy than brothers and sisters whose lives are more tranquil and secure. The need may be mental — extra tutoring, a special school. Or the need may be financial — expensive hobby equipment, a much-longed-for trip.

The more members there are in a family, the more difficult it is to appropriately weigh these varying needs and dispense available resources. But if parents deny the existence and the importance of

75

their children's varying needs, if they cannot be selectively and thoughtfully "inconsistent" at times, then the rigidity of their consistent treatment will be every bit as destructive as inconsistency normally is.

I can remember many examples in our own family when, for one reason or another, one daughter received "more" physical, moral, emotional, or financial support than did the others at the same time. But "more" for one wasn't perceived as deprivation or neglect by the others. They understood that we were simply responding, as parents, to needs we saw as vital. We explained our decision, insofar as that was appropriate, to the other children. And we found, over the years, that instead of being jealous that one sister had been given the money for a special series of lessons we thought would build her self-image, or that another sister was provided money for a trip to participate in something that would enrich her life, the other daughters felt reassured that when they had special needs, honest attempts to meet those needs would be made, without considering whether everyone else was getting similar treatment at the same time. What appeared to be inconsistent treatment was, in reality, consistent: a family policy of treating each person's needs as important was established, and that, I think, makes everyone feel secure. It certainly isn't always possible to meet the special needs our children have, or think they have, but when each knows that we are at least as willing to listen to him or her and consider the need, as we are to listen to the other children, then the whole family will feel secure.

*A third cause of parental inconsistency in applying discipline has to do with the situation:* the limits imposed by parents change with a change in location or a change of persons witnessing the child's behavior. For example, the parent who allows poor table manners at home suddenly becomes conscious of the child's deficiencies when dining somewhere else, and corrects behavior that has gone unnoticed at home. Or the parent who allows his or her children to be rude and disrespectful in their treatment of family members becomes embarrassed, angry, and punitive when the children treat valued guests in the same careless fashion.

Some situations and some people do require more formal, stylized manners and behavior than others. There is nothing inconsistent about that — the basic good manners are there, they are simply being utilized to a greater degree. But when very different behavior is tolerated, depending on where the child is, or with whom, first confusion, then resentment, results.

The confusion originates as the child tries to determine what really pleases the parent. Since the parent is not consistent in his or her demands, the child will not be able to make this determination. From confusion, resentment follows. Many a child who went willingly to visit relatives and friends, who looked forward to social gatherings, becomes completely negative to these same events when his or her "home" behavior is unacceptable, and publicly noted as such.

A possible further result of this type of inconsistency is that the child may detect underlying hypocrisy and an unchristian attitude in the parent who insists that certain people and certain events receive "better" treatment than others. The parable Christ told about the man seeking the highest place at the table and being sent down, while the man who chose a lowly place was invited to come up, certainly has something to say about social values. When, as parents, our treatment of others is determined by their identity or the situation, we are teaching our children to make judgments, assign values, and put people and places in a hierarchy of false importance based on external, nonessential matters. The worth of individuals lies not in how the public esteems them, but in the fact that they are loved by God. Surely, all friends of God should be treated with grace, respect, and kindness.

Possibly the most harmful result of discipline being rendered inconsistent by changing situations is that the child learns to develop an "image" rather than a "self." The behavior no longer honestly reflects the person, but is rather a mask to be used and discarded. A veneer of good behavior does no more to conceal the poor reality behind it than does one coat of stain on poorly grained wood.

*A fourth source of inconsistent discipline lies in the parents' understanding of the purpose of discipline.* The purpose of discipline, the reason limits are set, should be to enable each child to form internal controls, to assist the child in becoming an individual who can balance his or her wants and needs against those of others, and to help the child adapt to the requirements of social institutions. But some parents have very different ideas about why they discipline their children.

In the opening chapter of this book, I commented that, in many homes, the purpose of discipline is to provide a quiet atmosphere for the parents, and I discussed the ramifications of such a purpose. Some think that the purpose of discipline is to force the child to certain behavior, rather than to call it forth from within.

One or both of the parents may think that the purpose of discipline is to make the parent feel better about him- or herself. I know a large family in which every child was expected to take part in a competitive team sport and to begin training for that sport as early as possible. The training was year-round; during the school months, these children were driven to the gym at 6:30 AM so as to get in their practice for the day. There is no question that the children derived benefits from this sport. They have well-conditioned bodies, trained muscles, good respiratory and circulatory systems, and drawers and boxes of medals and trophies. They know how to work for goals, how to function as members of a team, how to win, and how to lose. All of these things are certainly beneficial.

The mother of the family had no freedom to schedule her own life, revolving as it did around the constant team meetings and practices of all her children. Since every child was engaged in the activity, it did not appear that they had a choice. I have only five children, and I doubt that they have ever unanimously chosen any one sport or activity with a duration of much more than one day. Individual needs and wants make it almost impossible for such unanimity to exist, even in a close family group. I still don't know why this family chose this way of life. I suspect that the parents knew that such activity would have the good results it did, and that they decided to seek those results in the same way for each child, no matter how different their children might be.

My disagreement with this approach is that it ignores the individuality of each child. A child is subjected to a form of discipline that may be uncomfortable, unpleasant, and distasteful, when another type of discipline could have the same good results. It is possible to have a well-conditioned body, trained muscles, good mental and physical health; to learn cooperation and to learn how to win and how to lose in many, many ways. Ballet dancers learn these things; so do tennis players, runners, actors, singers — even professional models spend hours a day in self-discipline. The solitary child who prefers to spend hours reading, thinking, and dreaming can become a walker — the best exercise of all.

What I am saying is that parents may choose poor means to reach good ends, and the choice may be interpreted as inconsistent by the children for whom the choice was made. "We are doing it for your own good," may make parents feel better about themselves, but for the child who sees only the immediate discomfort and not the long-range benefits or who knows very well there are other ways to reach those same good ends, the inconsistency is that the parents say they are thinking of the child's good, but the child feels that they are not.

A more insidious form of choosing methods of discipline to suit the parents' ends, rather than the child's ultimate good, results when the child becomes a weapon parents use against each other. One parent is cast as the "mean" parent, the other as the "kind" parent. The "kind" parent, in an effort to gain an ally against his or her "enemy," allows the child privileges outside the family disciplinary limits, conspires with the child to give him or her more "freedom," and generally undermines whatever understanding the child may have had about the real purpose of discipline and limits.

This type of behavior is generally the result of a deteriorating relationship between the parents. The "kind" parent may get enough gratification from having an ally against the other parent, and the hostile marital relationship may continue for years, with the children's maturation suffering greatly.

Of course, there are family situations in which the children need an ally, or, at least, a friend at court. With the best intentions in the world, a parent may make a decision involving the child that is simply not in the best interests of that child. Often, the decision concerns an area with moral, legal, or ethical implications. The conflict between the parent and the child then becomes more complicated, because if the parent feels he or she has God, the law, or an ethical code on his or her side, discussion and compromise will be difficult indeed.

Certainly, there are divine moral laws that cannot be compromised, and are not subject to opinion. But there are human laws which are not meant to be taken literally at all times. For example, in our city there is a law that teenagers under age seventeen may not drive after 11 PM, nor before 5 AM. The purpose of this law is to give law enforcement officials a valid reason to stop and question juveniles aimlessly driving around during these hours. So much juvenile crime occurs between 11 PM and 5 AM that the law is seen as a preventive measure. When it was passed by the city council, there was a certain amount of concern among teenagers and parents alike. School dances, private parties after football games, plays, band concerts, second features of movies—these events make an 11 PM curfew difficult to observe. And so the word was quietly put out by the Community Relations Department of the local police force that if teenagers under seventeen were driving home from a party or other legitimate activity, and were observing the laws concerning minors and alcohol, as well as the traffic laws, they would not be considered lawbreakers.

True, it is difficult to explain the varying shades

of legal grey that color our system of laws. But when parents, with the best intentions in the world, insist that their children obey laws such as this preventive curfew, there is likely to be trouble. The rigidity of the parent in being overly legalistic will result in the teenager's developing a negative attitude toward the parent's judgment.

It is in such a situation, when one parent has made such a decision, that the other parent may intervene on the part of the child. Private discussion between the two parents can lead to a change of decision. The new decision will be seen as more realistic and more in accord with the true needs of the child, who will gain in respect for an adult who can review a decision, revise it, and live with it. Children should not be given the idea that once a decision is made, one is irrevocably stuck with it.

There is quite a difference between forming a secret alliance with a child against the other parent, and acting as a liaison between conflicting parent and child. The second type of behavior is almost always positive, the first almost never is. But there are exceptions to every general statement, and there are rare occasions when an underground alliance may be valid. I remember the story about a woman, who, when she was a young girl, wanted to become a ballet dancer. Her father, a brilliant and successful attorney, would not hear of it. She was going to be a lawyer, and that was that. He was domineering, dictatorial, and impossible to deal with. The mother took the girl to ballet classes for years without the father knowing it. When it came time for the girl to begin college, instead of entering a university in pre-law, she auditioned for and was accepted by the Royal Ballet in London. She went on to become one of the world's great ballerinas.

It should be stressed that the above incident is unusual. Before a parent supports the interests and activities of a child against the will of the other parent, counseling is advisable. Such a lack of openness and mutuality in dealing with family problems should be considered only after the matter is examined as objectively as possible with outside trained help.

There will be inconsistency in discipline in every family. Because families are composed of imperfect human beings, there will be days when one child gets favored treatment, when children are chastised for behavior they never knew was unacceptable, and when parents indulge themselves in rule making for their own private ends. However, if there is an established system of discipline which the child understands and can depend upon to operate most of the time, the occasional inconsistency won't cause any real harm.

In any treatment of the issue of setting limits, of discipline as a means of enabling a child to develop internal controls, the problem of punishment must be addressed. I say the problem of punishment, for I consider it much more of a problem than a solution. The depressing statistics on penal populations, showing a higher and higher percentage of repeaters as age levels increase, demonstrate that punishment does not effectively change human behavior. People may obey the law from fear of being caught, but if that is their only motivation, the day will come when "being caught" seems improbable, and the good facade will crumble to reveal the poor foundation beneath.

Rehabilitation is one thing—punishment another. Rehabilitation programs, whether with children or adults, are quite different both in methods and purposes, from programs designed to "punish." I believe in rehabilitation, not punishment. I am well aware that there are criminals who cannot be rehabilitated to live nondestructively in an open society. But a very large percentage can be, and an even larger percentage could be rehabilitated, if punishment had not begun so early, had not in fact begun in the family. Rehabilitation, not punishment should be practiced in the family as well as in society at large. The growing interest in abused and battered children has led to studies that are discovering how many criminals as children were victims of deliberate punishment in the family.

The reason punishment is so widely used in the family is that beleagured parents often see no other way to achieve their goal of an obedient child. If the parental goal is to have a child who does what he or she is told, then punishment will surely help. If, however, the parental goal is to help the child become self-disciplined, punishment will rarely support that goal, and most often will actually work against it. If a parent punishes a child, that parent is doing something to the child that is painful and is causing the child to be unhappy. And no matter how loudly the parent proclaims, "This hurts me more than it does you," or "I am doing this only for your own good," the fact of the matter is that a child will find it very difficult to believe that he or she is loved if the parent continually uses pain, both emotional and physical, to change the child's behavior.

One of the first punishments a child is often subjected to is being sent to bed, or put alone in a room. I was fortunate enough to have a pediatrician who served as confidant and guide while I was becoming accustomed to motherhood. Before I ever brought the subject up, he said, "Never put a child to bed as punishment, and never put a small child in his or her room, away from the rest of the family, as punishment." He explained that good sleep habits are vital to good physical, mental, and emotional health. If a child associates going to bed with being punished, what sort of attitude toward sleep is being encouraged? As for isolating the child, he said that this feeds a small child's worst fear, the fear of separation from the parent. The feeling of isolation and loneliness, the anxiety, the feeling of rejection created in the young child by being shut up in a room, makes this punishment too severe for anything the child could do.

There are times when a child's misbehavior is the result of fatigue or overexcitement, and the child really does need a nap, or some time alone. My children were regularly sent to rest, or to calm down, when they were in these fatigued or overexcited states. The difference, as I see it, is not in what is done. It is in how it is done, and in what is said. Picture a mother suddenly swooping down on a screaming son, carrying him off to his room, dumping him unceremoniously on the bed, and shouting, "You're going to stay in here until you can behave!" and then slamming the door as she stomps out. To the boy this is seen as total rejection of himself, not as correction of his bad behavior.

There is a positive way to send a child to his or her room as a means of correcting misbehavior. A mother may be aware that her daughter is quarrelsome, whiny, or irritable, simply from being tired. The mother tells the girl that she has not gotten as much rest as she needs, that it isn't good for her to keep going when she is tired. She tells the child that she can choose to lie on her own bed, or on her mother's bed, or on the couch, or wherever, until she isn't so tired. The child will likely protest that she is not tired, to which the mother replies that she knows the child doesn't think she is tired, but since, when the child is rested, she doesn't lie on the floor and kick, doesn't throw toys around, doesn't whine, then obviously the child is tired and will feel much better after a rest. Most of the time the child is tired, will take a brief nap, and then return to play feeling much better. If the child isn't tired, but is simply acting out, the parent can count on the child being smart enough to figure out that the way to get out of bed is to abandon the misbehavior, announce that he or she is all rested, and start anew. If this sounds like playing games, so be it. At least it doesn't create an adversary situation; going to bed doesn't become a threat, and peace does descend.

Sending a child to his or her room as punishment can destroy what I believe to be one of the most valuable gifts we can give our children — the ability to re-create themselves in solitude. A child's room, whether shared with siblings or not, should be a place where he or she can go for private time, for thinking time, for the chance to just be.

Our girls have all shared bedrooms at one time or another; very seldom did anyone have a room of her own for any length of time. There was only one room available for single occupancy, and the girls took turns at having it as theirs. My husband built partitions; we bought screens and hung curtains; we did whatever it took to give each girl in her room some physical space in which to find emotional and mental and spiritual renewal.

If a child's room has such private space, the child will voluntarily seek that space when the going gets rough. The child will be the one stomping out of one room and into another, slamming and banging doors to express the pain and anger he or she won't or can't verbalize. How unfortunate it is when parents see this "retreat" as defiance, when they follow the child, bang on the door, and act as though they have been slapped or insulted. Our children must learn to deal with anger. They are going to have angry feelings all their lives. Storming off to his or her own room for a quieting-down time can be a means of handling anger. If we begin criticizing and judging the ways in which our children handle anger before they have had an opportunity to examine those ways themselves, we can do incalculable emotional harm. Repressed anger is beneath many neurotic and psychotic conditions, and the cause of much psychosomatic illness.

This really is the major problem with almost any kind of punishment. Instead of helping both parent and child deal with the anger or the hurt that the child's behavior is creating, punishment adds volatile fuel to the situation. The child's anger against the parent mounts, and the child becomes ever more self-righteous about his or her behavior.

The parent who has "brought up a very heavy gun to kill a very small sparrow," in turn becomes angry, not at the child, but at him- or herself for overreacting. The hurt remains, anger increases, and nothing is resolved.

There can be good discipline without punishment. It is a matter of enforcing a system in which privilege goes with responsibility. When definite privileges are tied to definite responsibilities, the child's failure to live up to the responsibility has the consequence of loss of a known privilege. The child knows this. The child chooses to lose the privilege if the child chooses to not accept the responsibility. If a teenager is allowed to use the car on the condition that it be returned by a certain hour, and if this agreement is clearly understood, then failure to return on time means that the teenager has chosen to run the risk of losing the privilege of using the car. If the weekly allowance is tied to certain household chores, on the theory that one who consumes contributes, then failure to perform those chores can be taken as evidence that the teenager or child would prefer to have less participation in the work of the family, and consequently, less sharing in the resources of the family. But such a system always allows for discussion, for the possibility of mutual effort at problem solving: "How can I help you live up to the agreement you made with me?" Such a method builds mutual trust and independent growth.

I feel that this system is much closer to the reality of the world than a system of punishments imposed by parents. Failure to perform tasks as an employee results in warnings, negative entries in the personnel file, and eventual job loss. The child who depends on someone else to "punish" him or her will either have to grow up very quickly or take some pretty hard falls when he or she is out there alone.

Another negative result of punishment is that the child who is punished for misbehavior may come to believe that he or she has "paid" for the crime, and may not learn anything about his or her reasons for choosing to behave in that way. The first step in controlling our behavior is to understand why we behave as we do. Victims of punishment imposed by others have difficulty taking that first step. They have been put into a state of pain by someone who professes to love them, which hardly makes them feel lovable. And if we suspect, deep down, that we are not lovable, we are frightened to look at ourselves, to examine ourselves, to know and finally accept ourselves. The freeing thing that Christ did for the people who thronged about him in his public ministry, and for all those who have believed in him in the centuries since his death, was to state clearly that God's love encompasses each and every human being, that God forgives all, and that we are not to be harder on ourselves than is God, who is the "parent" of us all. Christ's message is not that God sends people to eternal punishment; Christ's message is that people choose this for themselves by turning from God's love. I suspect that many more of our young people would understand this and incorporate it into their faith lives, if they grew up in families where "punishing" consequences were the result of one's own choices.

CHAPTER SIX
# The Question
# of Permissiveness

When one considers the many problems and awesome responsibilities that lie before new fathers and mothers as they begin parenthood, it is not totally surprising that recent polls report well over half the people queried said they would not have had children, had they known what parenthood was like. To compound the difficulty, one hears occasionally of an "adult" suing his or her parents for malpractice or incompetence.

Parenthood is difficult and certainly challenging, but few of life's really important endeavors are safe and easy. Despite talk about "overnight success" or "sudden rise to stardom" by writers, actors, singers, politicians, and other people thrust into the public eye, there is no such thing as instant success in any field. Success rests on work, on attention to detail, on faithful performance of necessary tasks, and on pure stubbornness to keep going no matter how tough it gets. Master carpenters have hammered many a crooked nail before they reached their high degree of proficiency; champion tennis players have hit many a ball into the net before they gained the control winning requires.

Whatever goal we set as our primary goal in life, that goal is going to take most of our energy, most of our time, most of our creative thinking, most of ourselves. There should be no higher priority for a mother or father than parenting a child. It is when parenthood conflicts with goals we consider more important that it becomes a burden. When parenting is seen as our primary task, when other activities are put in that perspective, then conflict is reduced; time is saved; energy and creative thinking are freed; and we may find, to our delight, that parenting is fun! Fun in the best sense, in that it re-creates us, brings joy, brings laughter, brings warmth, renews and restores us.

Recently, my youngest daughter, a young man, and I were visiting in the kitchen. I had had a particularly tiring week, involving a lot of physical tasks that I don't ordinarily do. As I set about preparing supper I was thinking that, if there were no hungry people coming home, I could eat cheese and fruit, soak in a hot tub, and pamper myself. Then I heard what my daughter was saying to her friend.

She was telling him about her first days at kindergarten, how reluctant she had been to go, and how much time I had spent with her getting her ready. "I remember Mama taking me to get material and patterns for the dresses she made, and for the smock I had to have. Do you remember that, Mama?" Did I remember! Going from one store to another with a five year old who very definitely knew what she liked and didn't like, finding patterns, finding material, and then fitting dresses on a wiggly little body that never seemed to be the same size two times running—how could I forget. "And then on the very second day," she went on, "I put on one of the dresses, but I really didn't want to go, and

91

Mama was getting dressed to take me, and I said — 'I don't want to go today,' and she said, 'Okay. You can come shopping with me.' "

I can't recall the emotions I had during those long-ago shopping trips with a five year old, but I do know what emotions I had on hearing her describe those experiences. Joy. Warmth. Reassurance, that despite our differences, despite the fact that we often stand toe-to-toe, parenting is worth all that we give it.

I've been describing a method of parenting that seeks to enable the child to make decisions and to take responsibility for the consequences of those decisions. My husband and I have rejected the authoritarian mode of parenting, and have allowed our daughters considerable freedom. To some this is "permissiveness," and they would cite the example of my letting my daughter go shopping with me rather than to school. But it seems to me that the type of parenting that is generally termed "permissive," and which is considered destructive, is not permissive at all. Such parenting is instead negligent, abandons parental responsibility, and excludes the child and his or her feelings from the parent's attention. In order to "permit" you to do something, I have to be aware of some responsibility to you, I have to know something about you, and what your capabilities and limitations are. The noun "permit" refers to an official document stating that certain activities are to be performed within certain limits. In the same way, I see the verb "permit" as guiding activities within certain limits which leave ample room for growth. Knowing my young daughter and aware of her needs, I "permitted" her to go shopping with me, rather than to school.

In a system of discipline which has as its goal

the development of individuals who have internal controls, who can balance their wants and needs against those of others, and who can adapt to the requirements of the social institutions in the larger world, we are immediately faced with the fact that each of the children to whom this system is applied will be different. Their genetic makeup will be different, their reactions to environmental influences will be different, and their reactions to the system will be different. I took all of this into account in permitting my daughter not to attend her second day of school.

The kind of permissiveness I'm talking about, the kind that I believe encourages each child's emotional, mental, and spiritual growth, involves an acceptance of the essential loneliness of every human being. We may have conceived our children, brought them into the world, nurtured them, cared for them, cheered for them, cried with them, but, as is the case with every human being, each child must take the full consequences of his or her behavior—alone. Friends may offer comfort, parents may offer help, but only the child can deal with the consequences. They are his or hers alone.

When we "permit" our children to operate in a system of discipline that sets definite limits, and yet is flexible in terms of how those limits are applied, when that system of discipline forces the child to accept the consequences of his or her own acts, own choices, then we are "permitting" that child to grow into a full human being, one who can meet life, who can not merely survive but who can live with joy. The strength to face life must come from within. External support will help, but can not substitute for internal controls and strengths.

We all know young people who will, for the rest of their lives, pay a terrible price for choices they have made. It may have been a choice to drive an automobile while drunk, or to get in a car driven by an intoxicated friend. The choice may have been to join the gang in breaking into a store "just this once," or to try heroin, or to risk pregnancy. There are young people who will live the rest of their days in wheelchairs, or on crutches, with facial scars, in blindness, or in prison, because they never learned the connection between choices they make and the consequences that are bound to follow.

One of my daughters told me, not too long ago, that when she was in her early teens she almost fell into the habit of lying to me about where she had been, what she had been doing. "There were things I wanted to do that I didn't think were wrong, but that I knew you wouldn't approve of," she said. "The other girls were lying about it, so I tried it, too. And then I remembered to whom I was lying. I remembered that you don't mind when I get angry at you, that you don't think I have to agree with you all the time, that you will listen, even if you don't always change your mind. And I decided that if I started lying to you, all that would end. Because I would be playing a game you've never played."

I was recently in traffic court with our youngest daughter; she hadn't come to a full stop at a stop sign. One young boy, only seventeen years old, had had his driver's license suspended on two prior occasions, but had continued to drive. Caught in another violation, he was told by the judge that he could not drive for three years, and his parents were told that if they allowed him to drive, the judge would fine them. The boy looked stunned. Obviously, despite his previous suspensions and his reactions to them, reactions which totally ignored the court's rulings, it had not occurred to him that such serious and long-lasting consequences would follow his bad choices.

Ultimately, each person must stand alone. Even if the parenting has been negligent, or the treatment of the child unfair, there must come a time when the responsibility for an individual's life is accepted by the one living it. Old behavior patterns can be changed and new ways can be learned. The ultimate choice to rise above the past, to survive, to live as productively as possible, is going to have to be up to the young person. He or she will have to make the choice, and implement it every day.

I really don't believe that children reared in rigid systems of discipline develop that kind of resilience. I don't believe they have come to accept, over years of trial and error, that though they err and make bad choices, the world will not cave in, they are still loved and loving human beings.

On the contrary a child raised in what I call a "permissive" system is able to develop the kind of positive self-love so vital to maturity. This child knows he or she is important and valued for the unique individual he or she is.

My mother followed such a system. So long as I maintained a normal pattern of carrying out school assignments and following through on commitments, she saw nothing wrong, if a time came when I was worn out, physically, emotionally, or mentally, in advising me to take the day off, to stay in bed, read, sip tea, dream, be. She did not see this as "being lazy and self-indulgent." She saw this as a way of helping me deal with the fact that no one will take better care of you than you will of yourself, and that if, early on, you do not learn that you are worth taking care of, you will probably lead a burdened life.

If total lack of self-discipline is harmful, the opposite, rigid self-discipline that requires superhuman performance at all times, is more harmful still. The "overachiever" never succeeds; always striving to live up to perfection, he or she is ever doomed to failure.

In a system of discipline built on a balance between privilege and responsibility, time off for good behavior comes very naturally. Why shouldn't the child who is caught up in schoolwork and who has earned the money to pay for it, take a day off to go see a special play or an exhibit, or to just enjoy life? The final result of self-discipline, it seems to me, is that an individual is in charge of his or her own life, can get necessary work done and yet make time for pleasure. By helping our children learn to take care of themselves even as they learn to discipline themselves, we are making a great contribution to their continued emotional and physical well-being.